THE FOREIGN SOURCES OF
SHAKESPEARE'S WORKS

THE FOREIGN SOURCES OF
SHAKESPEARE'S WORKS

An Annotated Bibliography
of the Commentary Written on this Subject
between 1904 and 1940
together with
Lists of Certain Translations
Available to Shakespeare

By SELMA GUTTMAN

1968
OCTAGON BOOKS, INC.
New York

016. 8223
G-98 f
68302

December, 1969

Reprinted 1968
by special arrangement with Selma Guttman
OCTAGON BOOKS, INC.
175 FIFTH AVENUE
NEW YORK, N. Y. 10010

LIBRARY OF CONGRESS CATALOG CARD NUMBER: 68-17374

Printed in U.S.A. by
NOBLE OFFSET PRINTERS, INC.
NEW YORK 3, N. Y.

TO MY MOTHER AND FATHER
WITH GRATITUDE

Contents

Introduction

FEW SHAKESPEAREAN PROBLEMS have occasioned greater divergence of opinion than the question of Shakespeare's learning. Had Ben Jonson been able to foresee the future, he would probably have blotted out some of his own lines and spared scholars the task of interpreting his still disputed reference to Shakespeare's knowledge of the classics:

> And though thou hadst small Latine and lesse Greeke
> From thence to honour thee, I would not seeke
> For names; but call forth thund'ring Aeschilus,
> Euripides, and Sophocles to us.
> Paccuuius, Accius, him of Cordova dead,
> To life againe, to heare thy Buskin tread,
> And shake a Stage . . .

Those lines cause just as bitter a controversy today as they did one hundred and eighty years ago when Richard Farmer published *An Essay on the Learning of Shakespeare*. Reacting against the exaggerated claims of Shakespeare's great learning advanced by such critics as John Upton and Peter Whalley, Farmer reverted to the misinterpretation fostered by members of the tribe of Ben, who had chosen to exalt the erudition and wisdom of Jonson by denying any book learning whatsoever to Shakespeare. Like them, Farmer maintained that Shakespeare was ignorant of both the classical and the continental tongues. His thesis was so widely accepted as to stimulate Samuel Johnson to observe: "Dr. Farmer . . . you have done that which never was done before; that is, you have completely finished a controversy beyond all further doubt."[1]

Dr. Johnson, however, was not omniscient, for the controversy continued. Fresh stimulus was added to it in 1857 when Delia S. Bacon published *The*

1. James Northcote, *Memoirs of Sir Joshua Reynolds, Knt.,* Philadelphia, 1817, p. 78.

Philosophy of the Plays of Shakespeare Unfolded, a book in which she proposed Francis Bacon as the real author of the Shakespeare canon. Since Bacon was one of the most learned of the Elizabethans, this suggestion was enthusiastically hailed by those classically-minded scholars who still heard echoes of antiquity in Shakespeare's lines. They used the Baconian authorship of the plays as justification for their enthusiastic, and frequently undiscriminating, collection of parallels between Shakespeare and the classics. Indeed, the collection of such parallels became a popular sport among Baconians and non-Baconians alike during the latter part of the nineteenth and the early part of the twentieth century. One of the most noteworthy essays of this period was written by a non-Baconian, John Churton Collins. His essay, "Shakespeare as a Classical Scholar," first appeared in *The Fortnightly Review* in 1903 and was reprinted in a collection of his essays: *Studies in Shakespeare,* Westminster, 1904. After surveying the earlier criticism on the subject of Shakespeare's learning and analyzing the course of study of the Ipswich Grammar School in 1528, Collins effectively supported the thesis that Shakespeare had probably read in the original Latin such authors as Ovid, Plautus, and Seneca. Thus far, Collins' approach meets with the approval of present-day scholars. Unfortunately, however, when urging Shakespeare's familiarity with Greek drama in Latin translation, he weakened his thesis by listing many insignificant parallels which, as he himself acknowledged, could have been the result of pure coincidence or of an indirect, rather than a direct, influence upon Shakespeare.

The listing of classical parallels was carried *ad absurdum* by such critics as William Theobald, who, in *The Classical Element in the Shakespeare Plays,* London, 1909, sought to prove Shakespeare's classicism by the sheer number rather than by the validity of his parallels. Some of the more modern critics have still clung to this method, as can be seen by examining commentary written by J. E. Johnstone[2] and R. P. Cowl. The following insignificant parallel, for example, is cited by Cowl:

> North's Plutarch "Fabius":
> "Wherefore consider what you have to do."
> *The First Part of King Henry the Fourth,* V, ii, 77:
> "Better consider what you have to do."[3]

In *The Baconian Heresy,* London, 1913, J. M. Robertson systematically and,

2. J. E. Johnstone, "The Classical Element in Shakespeare," *The Catholic World,* 106 (1917): 38-52.
3. [R. P. Cowl] *Sources of the Text of Henry the Fourth,* Bruges, 1928, p. 40.

on the whole, effectively attacked such scholars as Collins and Theobald by suggesting continental and English sources for many of the so-called recondite classicisms which they had enumerated. Unfortunately, Robertson later over-stepped the mark and, devoting himself to the disintegration of the Shake-speare canon, denied the Shakespearean authorship of certain passages and plays which smacked too strongly of classical allusion.

It is, in part, due to the labors of such men that the philosophy of Baconianism and the method of scholarship fostered by the Baconians have fallen into disrepute. For the downfall of Baconianism some credit must also be given to the more rabid members of the Baconian cult whose exaggerations have proved the untenability of their position. Some of them have suggested that Bacon wrote not only Shakespeare's works but also the choice works of such writers as Marlowe, Greene, Lyly, Spenser, Kyd, and Burton. The Ba-conians have fallen into such disrepute that some critics tend to forget the valuable contribution which this group has made to Shakespearean study. It cannot be denied that the Baconians were among the first to awaken modern critics to the significance of the classical influence upon Shakespeare. Today there are few critics who distort Jonson's "small Latine" into "no Latin at all." Neither, on the other hand, are there many who, going to the opposite extreme, interpret Jonson to have meant that Shakespeare was deeply learned and that his "though thou hadst small Latine and lesse Greeke" was intended as a subjunctive contrary to fact.

The leading critics of today approach the problem from a new perspective. They seek to discover just what a learned man of the English Renaissance would have meant by the term "small Latine." They conclude that in the days of good Queen Bess those words would have embraced far more than they do today. In other words, modern critics are attempting to study Shakespeare in historical perspective, to further their understanding of a literary genius by examining the intellectual milieu in which he thrived.

They point to the important rôle that the classical tongues played in the sixteenth century. The scholarship of such secretaries of King Henry VII as Polydore Vergil and of King Henry VIII as Andrea Ammonio shows that Latin, which had been the universal language of the Middle Ages, was still of the highest importance in diplomacy. That Latin was still the universal language of the scholar is obvious from the fact that Erasmus, who spoke no English, was able to enjoy intellectual association with native scholars during his several visits to England. The scholarly attainments of such persons as Lady Jane Grey and of Queen Elizabeth herself also testify to the importance of the classics. Nor must we conclude that such familiarity with the classics was the exception, for the works of Shakespeare and of the other Elizabethan playwrights and novelists would not be so replete with classical allusions if such allusions had not struck a familiar note in the ear of their audiences.

E. M. W. Tillyard, in *Shakespeare's History Plays,* London, 1944, has pointed out, moreover, that Shakespeare's plays contain intellectual concepts similar to those found in the works of the learned Spenser and Sidney, concepts which were derived, at least originally, from fairly recondite sources. Since Shakespeare used such ideas to illustrate the subject at hand rather than to parade his own knowledge, Tillyard has concluded that Shakespeare had a far greater store of knowledge than he utilized in his plays.

Tillyard's picture of Shakespeare in the center of the intellectual currents of his day would be not only unacceptable but also ludicrous if one retained the old conception of Stratford-on-Avon as an unclean and bookless country town. Today's critics, however, following the lead of J. S. Smart,[4] visualize sixteenth-century Stratford as a thriving metropolis, in which Shakespeare's father for several years served as Chamberlain and kept town records, in which Richard Quiney received a letter written in Latin by his eleven-year-old son, Richard Junior, and in which young children received copies of works by Aesop, Erasmus, Cicero, Sallust, Justin, Vergil, and Horace, that were bequeathed to them by their Vicar, John Brechtgirdle.

The biographical legends concerning the young Shakespeare, himself, have also been re-evaluated. The trend today is to accept John Aubrey's statement (derived from William Beeston) that Shakespeare "had been in his younger yeares a Schoolmaster in the Countrey" rather than Dowdall's report that Shakespeare had been apprenticed to a butcher. Recent studies have been made, too, of the typical grammar school curricula in Elizabethan England, and in a painstaking work, *William Shakspere's Small Latine and Lesse Greeke,* Urbana, 1944, T. W. Baldwin has utilized such information to help ascertain the classical works (and in some instances the probable editions of those works) which Shakespeare probably used at school. His list is both impressive and plausible.[5] What Shakespeare read of the classics after he had

---

4. J. S. Smart, *Shakespeare: Truth and Tradition,* London, 1928.

5. Among Shakespeare's probable school texts, Baldwin discusses the following: Aesop's *Fables* in Latin, edited by Camerarius; Aphthonius' *Progymnasmata* translated into Latin by Rudolphus Agricola and Johannes M. Cataneus with the scholia of R. Lorichius; Cicero's *Ad Herennium* edited by Lambinus; Cicero's *Topica, Tusculan Disputations, Epistles;* Cooper's *Thesaurus;* Culmann's *Sententiae pueriles;* Erasmus' *Adagia, Copia, Colloquia, De conscribendis;* Horace's *Odes* and, probably, *Ars poetica,* both edited by Lambinus; probably several satires by Juvenal; Lilly's Latin Grammar; some passages from Livy; perhaps some Lucian in Latin or Greek; Mantuan's *Eclogues* with the notes by Badius; Mirandula's *Flores poetarum;* Ovid's *Fasti, Heroides,* and *De tristibus* in Latin; Ovid's *Metamorphoses* in the Latin with the notes of Regius and also in the Golding translation; Palingenius' *Zodiacus vitae;* probably some of

completed his schooling cannot be so closely approximated. Indeed, there is little possibility that absolute agreement on either of these problems will ever be achieved.

Nor is there more probability that complete agreement will ever be attained on the question of Shakespeare's familiarity with French and Italian.[6] Some critics, still following the dictum of Farmer, categorically deny that Shakespeare was familiar with the works of Montaigne prior to 1603, the date of Florio's English translation of the *Essais*. At the opposite extreme, one finds critics who offer philosophical parallels between Montaigne and Shakespeare as incontrovertible proof that Florio and Shakespeare were pseudonyms for Francis Bacon. The majority of critics today take the middle ground. Since Shakespeare's use of French in his plays demonstrates that he had a colloquial acquaintance with the language, they assume that, with his knowledge of Latin, he would have been able to read at least some French.

Shakespeare's classical background is also used to support the contention that he would not have found it very difficult to obtain a reading knowledge of Italian. His interest in this language might also have been whetted by association in London with such men as John Florio. Florio, who became Reader in Italian to Queen Anne, had compiled books of English and Italian dialogues as well as an Italian-English dictionary for the student of Italian. Since both he and Shakespeare enjoyed the patronage of Southampton, it is well within the realm of possibility that they were acquainted. In London, too, Shakespeare would have had the opportunity of seeing travelling Italian companies present *commedie dell' arte*. Indeed, critics have recently shown much interest in the possible influence of the *commedia dell' arte* upon Shakespeare's own comedies.

The similarity between certain Shakespearean plots and Italian *novelle* has long been realized. It is true that most critics consider George Whetstone's extant English play, *Promos and Cassandra,* a more significant source of *Measure for Measure* than its original, a *novella* by Giraldi Cintio,[7] or than Giraldi's dramatization of that *novella: Epitia.* However, some of the similari-

Persius' satires; Plautus' comedies edited by Lambinus; Pliny edited by Dalechampius; Quintillian's *Institutio oratoria*; Susenbrotus' *Epitome troporum*; Terence's comedies, probably edited by Willichius; Textor's *Epitheta* and similar works; Udall's *Floures for Latin Spekynge Selected and Gathered out of Terence*; Vergil's *Aeneid* I-VI, probably with the notes of Willichius and Servius; perhaps Vives' *Satellitum* and *Introductio ad sapientam*; and Withal's *Little Dictionarie.*

6. Despite the strenuous efforts of Joseph de Perott, the general consensus of opinion today is that Shakespeare's knowledge of Spanish classics was small and was derived through translation. Few critics, if any, have seriously considered the possibility of Shakespeare's direct knowledge of German literature.

7. Fifth tale of the eighth decade of *Hecatommithi.*

ties between Shakespearean and Italian works cannot be explained away so easily. For example, no English analogue is extant which could have served in lieu of Giraldi as the source of *Othello*.[8] According to Werner Wokatsch, this fact cannot be evaded satisfactorily by referring to the French translation by Gabriel Chappuys, since Shakespeare utilized a phrase which is to be found in the Italian but not in the French version.[9] Because of slight discrepancies between the versions of Shakespeare and of Giraldi, A. H. Krappe has tried to discard Giraldi as the source of *Othello* in favor of some other, unknown, cognate of Giraldi,[10] but his hypothesis has not found general favor.

It is especially tempting to follow this method of Krappe when one is considering a Shakespearean play that contains the distinctive characteristics of several of its analogues. Although a *novella* by Boccaccio,[11] for instance, is the closest analogue to *Cymbeline* yet discovered, a number of *Cymbeline's* analogues, including the two English tales: *Frederick of Jennen* (a translation of *Die Historie von vier Kaufmännern*, a cognate of Boccaccio's tale) and the second tale of *Westward for Smelts* contain some parallels to Shakespeare not to be found in Boccaccio. W. F. Thrall, therefore, has suggested that both *Cymbeline* and the two English versions were derived from some common source which has since been lost.[12] Generally, however, the practice today is to frown upon such hypotheses because, although they cannot be categorically refuted, neither can they be satisfactorily proved.

A very different solution to a similar problem has been suggested by Morton Luce. He observed interesting similarities between *Twelfth Night* and a number of its analogues. Instead of suggesting Shakespeare's dependence upon some lost and unknown work, Luce concluded that Shakespeare utilized a number of the versions available to him: Barnabe Rich's "Of Apolonius and Silla," several Italian comedies, the versions in Bandello and in Belleforest, and, perhaps, additional sources as well.[13]

It must, of course, be realized that even in those cases in which Shake-

8. Seventh tale of the third decade of *Hecatommithi*.

9. Werner Wokatsch, "Zur Quelle des *Othello* und zu Shakespeares Kenntnis des Italienischen," *Archiv für das Studium der neueren Sprachen und Literaturen*, 162 (1932): 118-119. Giraldi has "*se non mi fai . . . vedere cogl' occhi.*" The French version reads: "*si tu ne me fais voir.*" In *Othello* we find: "Give me the ocular proof. . . . Make me to see't" (*Othello*, III, iii, 361, 365).

10. A. H. Krappe, "A Byzantine Source of Shakespeare's *Othello*," *Modern Language Notes*, 39 (1924): 156-161.

11. Ninth Tale on the Second Day of *The Decameron*.

12. W. F. Thrall, "*Cymbeline*, Boccaccio, and the Wager Story in England," *Studies in Philology*, 28 (1931): 639-651.

13. *Rich's Apolonius and Silla: An Original of Shakespeare's Twelfth Night*, ed. Morton Luce, London, 1912, xii, 96 pp.

speare's actual sources can be determined beyond question, there may be discrepancies between the original and Shakespeare's finished product. Modern critics have, therefore, been interested in analyzing Shakespeare's manipulation of his sources in order to obtain a better understanding not only of Shakespeare's dramatic technique, but also of Shakespearean passages which, hitherto, have puzzled or shocked the commentators. That personal predilection and poetic insight in some cases, and stage requirements in others, caused Shakespeare to revise some material is evident. Shakespeare also frequently found it necessary to revise the material he borrowed in order to make it palatable to Renaissance morality and culture. This is true, to cite two fairly obvious instances, of his characterizations of Bertram in *All's Well That Ends Well* and of Adriana in *The Comedy of Errors.*

Sometimes, Shakespeare blended his main source with interpretations derived from later literature. As H. M. Ayres has demonstrated, Shakespeare's deviations from the Plutarchan conception of Julius Caesar were due to the influence of pseudo-Senecan, Renaissance plays written about Caesar.[14] J. S. P. Tatlock has shown that Shakespeare deviated from the Boccaccian and Chaucerian interpretations of Cressida, not because he wished to express personal disillusionment (although earlier critics have so maintained), but because the character of Cressida had been degraded in late medieval and in Renaissance story.[15] O. J. Campbell has noted further that, since Shakespeare was trying his hand at dramatic satire, the degraded Cressida of later legend was more suitable to his purposes.[16]

In still other cases, it is Shakespeare's adherence to his source, rather than his deviation therefrom, that has caused difficulty for the commentators. The modern world is so far removed from medieval tradition that several of Shakespeare's plays have been very puzzling to readers no longer aware of the conventions of the medieval tales of virtue upon which Shakespeare was depending. By comparing the conventions of this literary genre with some of Shakespeare's plays, W. W. Lawrence has aided immeasurably in clarifying Shakespeare's intention in these plays.[17]

It must not be assumed that modern criticism has solved all the problems connected with Shakespeare's sources. This is far from the case. It is felt,

14. H. M. Ayres, "Shakespeare's *Julius Caesar* in the Light of Some Other Versions," *PMLA*, 25 (1910): 183-227.

15. J. S. P. Tatlock, "The Chief Problem in Shakespeare," *Sewanee Review*, 24 (1916): 129-147; and "The Siege of Troy in Elizabethan Literature, Especially in Shakespeare and Heywood," *PMLA*, 30 (1915): 673-770.

16. O. J. Campbell, *Comicall Satyre and Shakespeare's* Troilus and Cressida, San Marino, Cal., 1938.

17. W. W. Lawrence, *Shakespeare's Problem Comedies*, New York, 1931.

however, that an examination of modern criticism will aid the student not only by giving him a picture of present-day attitudes on these questions, but also by prompting him to undertake the unravelling of source problems yet unsolved. It is for these reasons that this bibliography of commentary on Shakespeare's sources has been undertaken. In preparing a work of this sort, one is torn between two desiderata: selectivity and objectivity. Because (as has been demonstrated) there is so much disagreement on the subject of Shakespearean sources, objectivity seemed the more pressing need. Hence, no attempt has been made to separate the wheat from the chaff, and some of the source suggestions herein recorded are implausible and far-fetched.

This study begins with 1904, the date of H. R. D. Anders' *Shakespeare's Books,* and extends up to 1940. It deals with English, French, and German commentary concerning Shakespearean sources originally written in foreign languages. Classified according to the original language of each of the works influencing Shakespeare, the material in this annotated bibliography is further subdivided alphabetically according to the authorship of the sources. Preceding the opinions regarding Shakespeare's use of each source are lists of certain translations available to Shakespeare.

Since absolute completeness in a bibliography of this sort would be both impossible and undesirable, certain general limitations have been set. Only those foreign sources which directly influenced works in Shakespeare's accepted canon are considered. Neither Shakespearean sources written in a foreign tongue by an English author nor works written in English but first printed abroad fall within the scope of this study. Commentary on Shakespeare's knowledge of law, medicine, biology and the Bible are omitted. The critical commentary to be included has been further limited by the following considerations:

1. Denials of Shakespeare's use of a source are rarely included except when the affirmative point of view is also recorded.
2. Some of the more cursory comments and critical reviews are omitted, especially in the case of such widely accepted sources as Ovid, Plutarch, Montaigne, and Boccaccio.
3. Source suggestions contained in lives of Shakespeare and in editions of Shakespeare's works are not considered, because of their general dependence upon earlier tradition.
4. Later editions of criticisms that were originally written before 1904 are usually omitted.

5. Rudolf Grossman's *Spanien und das elisabethanische Drama,* Hamburg, 1920, is not included because of its unwieldy arrangement.

6. The following works contain a profusion of highly questionable Shakespearean sources, including many Greek works which were untranslated in the Elizabethan age:

[R. P. Cowl] *Sources of the Text of Henry the Fourth;* William Theobald, *The Classical Element in the Shakespeare Plays;* and J. E. Johnstone, "The Classical Element in Shakespeare." For this reason, suggestions found only in these works are omitted.[18]

In some criticisms, on the other hand, possible sources are discarded too summarily. H. M. Blake, for example [see entry 293] discards Lucian as a source on the grounds that those works of Lucian which have been suggested as Shakespeare's sources were unavailable in English. Yet, there are sixteenth-century versions of Lucian in Latin, French, Italian, Spanish, and German. These Blake ignores. Such neglect by certain critics suggested the need for lists of Renaissance translations. Since the purpose of these lists is to demonstrate in how many different versions Shakespeare could have read each source, only one edition of each translation is cited. In order to avoid possible duplication, those editions which lack the name of the translator, and which I have not been able to examine, are usually omitted. Except in a very few instances, it is futile to hazard even a guess as to the specific edition which Shakespeare might have used. In such cases, I have listed one of the possible editions upon which the dramatist might have depended.

It is assumed that Shakespeare, wherever possible, would have availed himself of the original or of an English translation; therefore, when English versions of a source have been found, the foreign translations are usually omitted. The lists make no attempt to include all those works, of any given author, which did not have a direct influence upon Shakespeare. Only *bona fide* translations are stressed; plagiarisms and adaptations are rarely mentioned. Translations in manuscript and hypothetical printed translations are generally omitted. Since stress is laid upon different translations rather than upon the editions of those translations, and since many rare volumes of translations were not accessible for personal inspection, the title pages are not completely reproduced. Only the essential portions of the titles are given. Where the original author's name appears as part of the title, it is omitted. When no translations are recorded, the reader is to assume that this bibliographer has found none which might have been available to Shakespeare.

In the annotated entries, the following bibliographical procedure is used. A

18. For bibliographical data on these works, see entries 15, 9, and 16 respectively.

uniform system of punctuation within titles is used. Complete bibliographical data are given only once, a system of cross-reference being used. An independent system of cross-reference is used in the annotations proper, when such cross-reference is deemed necessary. In the annotations, quotations from Shakespeare's works and the line references to them are made to conform with the one-volume Oxford edition of W. J. Craig.

Without the unfailing encouragement and assistance of Professor Oscar James Campbell, of Columbia University, this work could never have been completed. I am deeply indebted to Dr. Samuel A. Tannenbaum, editor of the *Shakespeare Association Bulletin,* who generously placed at my disposal his library and certain unpublished bibliographical data. To Professor Percy W. Long, Secretary of the Modern Language Association, I wish to express my gratitude for many valuable suggestions. For detailed examination of my manuscript, I am very grateful to Professors Elliott Van Kirk Dobbie, Dino Bigongiari, Robert Herndon Fife and Susanne H. Nobbe and to Doctors Henry W. Wells and Nathan Edelman of Columbia University as well as to Miss Constance Winchell and Mr. Thomas P. Fleming of the Columbia University Library. My research has been immeasurably facilitated by the unfailing cooperation of the reference staffs of the following libraries: Columbia University Library, New York Public Library, the Library of the University of Wisconsin and of the Historical Society of the State of Wisconsin, and the Library of the University of Kansas. I wish to take the opportunity here to express my appreciation for the assistance which I have received from many other friends in New York, at the University of Wisconsin, and at the University of Kansas.

List of Bibliographies

Information regarding the translations available to Shakespeare was culled from the following bibliographies:

Antonio, Nicolás, *Bibliotheca hispana nova, sive Hispanorum scriptorum, qui ab anno MD. ad MDCLXXXIV floruere notitia,* Madrid, 1783-1788.

——— *Bibliotheca hispana vetus, sive, Hispani scriptores qui ab Octaviani Augusti aevo ad annum Christi MD. floruerunt,* Madrid, 1788.

Bibliothèque nationale, *Catalogue général des livres imprimés,* Paris, 1900-1934.

British Museum, *Catalogue of Books in the Library of the British Museum Printed in England, Scotland, and Ireland, and of English Books Printed Abroad to the Year 1640,* London, 1884.

——— *Catalogue of Printed Books,* London, 1881-1900; Supplement, 1900-1905.

Brunet, Gustave, *La France littéraire au XV* siècle, ou Catalogue raisonné des ouvrages en tout genre imprimés en langue française jusqu'à l'an 1500,* Paris, 1865.

Brunet, J. C. *Manuel du libraire et de l'amateur de livres,* Paris, 1860-1865.

Copinger, W. A., *Supplement to Hain's Repertorium bibliographicum, or Collection toward a New Edition of That Work,* London, 1895-1902.

La Croix du Maine et Du Verdier, *Les Bibliothèques Françoises de la Croix du Maine et de Du Verdier, revue, corrigée et augmentée par M. Rigoley de Juvigny,* Paris, 1773.

Ebert, F. A., *General Bibliographical Dictionary* [tr. from German by Arthur Browne], Oxford, 1837.

Gesammtkatalog der Wiegendrucke, ed. *Kommission für den Gesammtkatalog der Wiegendrucke,* Leipzig, 1925-1940.

Haebler, Konrad, *Bibliografía ibérica del siglo XV. Enumeración de todos los libros impresos en España y Portugal hasta el año de 1500 con notas críticas,* The Hague, 1903.

Hain, L. F. T., *Reportorium bibliographicum ad annum MD.,* Stuttgart, 1826-1838.

Heredia y Livermore, Ricardo, conde de Benhavis, *Catalogue de la bibliothèque de M. Ricardo Heredia,* Paris, 1891-1894.

John Rylands Library, *Catalogue of the Printed Books and Manuscripts in the John Rylands Library,* Manchester, 1899.

Lanson, Gustave, *Manuel bibliographique de la littérature française moderne 1500-1900,* Paris, 1914.

Lonchamp, F. C., *Manuel du bibliophile français (1470-1920)*, Paris and Lausanne, 1927, vol. 2.

Lowndes, W. T., *The Bibliographer's Manual of English Literature*, London, 1857.

Maggs Brothers, *Books Printed in France and French Books Printed in Other Countries from 1470 to 1700 A.D.*, London, 1926.

────── *Books Printed in Spain and Spanish Books Printed in Other Countries*, London, 1927.

Nijhoff, Wouter, and M. E. Kronenberg, *Nederlandsche bibliographie van 1500 tot 1540*, The Hague, 1923-1924.

Panzer, G. W. F., *Annalen der ältern deutschen Litteratur*, Nuremberg, 1788-1805.

Penney, C. L., *List of Books Printed before 1601 in the Library of the Hispanic Society of America*, New York, 1929.

────── *List of Books Printed 1601-1700 in the Library of the Hispanic Society of America*, New York, 1938.

Pollard, A. W. and G. R. Redgrave, *Short-Title Catalogue of Books Printed in England, Scotland, and Ireland and of English Books Printed Abroad, 1475-1640*, London, 1926.

Salvá y Mallen, D. Pedro, *Catálogo de la biblioteca de Salvá*, Valencia, 1872.

Thomas, Henry, *Short Title Catalogue of Books Printed in Spain and of Spanish Books Printed Elsewhere in Europe before 1601 Now in the British Museum*, London, 1921.

────── with the assistance of A. F. Johnson and A. G. Macfarlane, *Short Title Catalogue of Books Printed in France and of French Books Printed in Other Countries from 1470 to 1600 Now in the British Museum*, London, 1924.

Abbreviations

RJ	Romeo and Juliet
TS	The Taming of the Shrew
Tem	The Tempest
Timon	Timon of Athens
TC	Troilus and Cressida
Titus	Titus Andronicus
TN	Twelfth Night or What You Will
TGV	The Two Gentlemen of Verona
VA	Venus and Adonis
WT	A Winter's Tale

Magazines*

A	Anglia, Zeitschrift für Englische Philologie
Ar	Archiv für das Studium der neueren Sprachen und Literaturen
ESn	Englische Studien
MLN	Modern Language Notes
MLR	Modern Language Review
MP	Modern Philology
N	Nation
19 C	Nineteenth Century and After
NQ	Notes and Queries
PQ	Philological Quarterly
PMLA	Publications of the Modern Language Association of America
RES	Review of English Studies
RLC	Revue de littérature comparée
SAB	Shakespeare Association Bulletin
SJ	Jahrbuch der Deutschen Shakespearegesellschaft
SP	Studies in Philology
TLS	Times Literary Supplement

Miscellaneous

B	Bulletin
CL	Columbia University Library
ed	edited by
introd.	introduction by

* For the abbreviation of a portion of a magazine title see under miscellaneous abbreviations.

J .... Journal
L .... Library
MS .... Manuscript
n.d. .... date unknown
no pl. .... place unknown
no tr. .... translator unknown
Q .... Quarterly
R .... Review
S .... Shakespeare
Sn .... Shakespearean
Sna .... Shakespeareana
tr. .... translator, or translated by
U .... University

CHAPTER ONE

Influence of Latin Literature on Shakespeare

Aegidius Romanus, see **Colonna, Egidio**

Agrippa, Cornelius

(1)

Koszul, A., "Ariel," *English Studies,* Amsterdam, 19 (1937): 200-204.

The name, Ariel, might have been derived from Cornelius Agrippa's *De occulta philosophia,* although whether directly or indirectly is uncertain.

Albertus Magnus

ENGLISH: *The Boke of Secretes* [no tr.], London [1560?].

(2)

Jaggard, William, *Shakespeare Once a Printer and Bookman,* Stratford on Avon, 1933, p. 8.

Albertus Magnus' *Boke of Secretes* appears to be the source of *AC,* I, ii, 10 ("In nature's infinite book of secrecy").

Alciatus, Andreas

FRENCH: *Livret des emblemes* [tr. J. Le Fevre], Paris, 1536.
Emblemes [tr. Barth. Aneau], Lyons, 1549.
[*Les Emblèmes,* tr. Claude Mignaut, Paris, 1584.]
ITALIAN: *Diverse imprese accommodate a diverse moralità . . . tratte dagli emblemi* [by Giovanni Marquale], Lyons, 1549.
SPANISH: *Los emblemas* [tr. B. Daza], Lyons, 1549.
GERMAN; . . . *Emblematum libellus,* tr. W. Hunger, Paris, 1542.
Liber emblematum, tr. J. Held, Frankfort on Main, 1580.

(3)

Fairchild, A. H. R., "A Note on *Macbeth*," PQ, 4 (1925) : 348-350.

The picture and the lines under Alciatus' *Emblema*, XVI (as given in the Leyden edition of 1608) were in S's mind when he wrote *Mac*, I, iv, 52 ("The eye wink at the hand . . .").

Apuleius, Lucius

ENGLISH: *The XI Bookes of the Golden Asse*, tr. W. Adlington, London, 1566.

(4)

Anders, H., "*The Golden Asse* of Lucius Apuleius . . . with an Intro-
    duction by E. B. Osborn . . . ," SJ, 62 (1926) : 172-173.

Apuleius' use of the ass suggested to S the idea of Bottom's metamorphosis. The Cupid in *The Golden Asse*, XXII, was the forerunner of Puck. Chapter XXV of the same work was the source of *WT*, IV, iii, 816 ff. ("He has
a son, who shall be flayed . . ."). [In his edition, E. B. Osborn does not
consider the question of S's indebtedness to Apuleius.]

(5)

Buchin, Erna, "Sidney's *Arcadia* als Quelle für *Cymbeline*," Ar, 143
    (1922) : 250-252.

Hermann Reich's thesis that Apuleius' *Golden Asse* influenced *Cym* is
considered, but Sidney's *Arcadia* is preferred as a more probable source of
the Sn play. See 8.

(6)

Haight, E. H., *Apuleius and His Influence*, New York, 1927, p. 140.

Although one is tempted to find echoes of Apuleius' *Golden Asse* in *MND*,
there is no evidence of S's having borrowed from this source.

(7)

Reich, Hermann, "Der Mann mit dem Eselkopf: Ein Mimodrama vom
    klassischen Altertum verfolgt bis auf Shakespeare," SJ, 40 (1904):
    108-128.

Resemblances between the ass scenes of *MND* and Apuleius' *Golden
Asse* are noted. S might have received additional suggestions for Bottom's
metamorphosis from puppet plays and interludes.

(8)

Reich, Hermann, "Zur Quelle des *Cymbelin*," *SJ*, 41 (1905) : 177-181.

The scenes in *Cym* depicting Imogen in the presence of her stepmother, Imogen's sojourn in the forest cave, her being poisoned and the results thereof were all derived from Apuleius' *Golden Asse*. See 5.

(9)

Theobald, William, *The Classical Element in the Shakespeare Plays*, ed. R. M. Theobald, London, 1909, pp. 76-78.

Apuleius was the source of lines in *Cym, TC,* and *WT*.

Baptista Mantuanus [pseudonym for Battista Spagnuoli]

Although almost every survey of S's sources includes Mantuan's *Eclogues* as one of S's school texts and points out its influence on *LLL* and *MW*, no detailed discussion of this source occurs within the period covered by this bibliography. See also Introduction, footnote 5.

Saint Bernard

Since G. P. Smith believes that S was probably influenced by the original Latin of Saint Bernard, translations are not cited here.

(10)

Smith, G. P., "A Note to Lines 18-20, Act II, Sc. i of *As You Like It*," *A*, 56 (1932) : 318-320.

AYL, II, i, 15 ff. ("And this our life . . .") was probably derived from the following Latin passage of St. Bernard: *"Experto crede: aliquid amplius invenies in silvis . . ."* (in *Opera genuina*, Paris, 1845, *Epistola* CVI, 2, p. 95) or from a collection of *sententiae* culled from St. Bernard's writings.

Boccaccio, *De casibus virorum* is included with the Italian works.

Caesar, Julius

ENGLISH: *Julius Cesars Commentaryes*, tr. J. Tiptoft, London, 1530. *The Eyght Bookes of . . . Caesar*, tr. A. Goldinge, London, 1565.

Lists of S's probable school texts frequently include Caesar's *Commentaries*.

(11)

Jaggard, William, *Shakespeare Once a Printer and Bookman,* p. 10. See 2.

Caesar is mentioned by name in *AYL,* V, ii, 35 and in *2H6,* IV, vii, 59.

(12)

Sandys, J. E., "Scholarship" in *Shakespeare's England,* Oxford, 1916, I: 251-283. [Caesar, p. 264.]

The description of Kent in *2H6,* IV, vii, 65, can not serve as proof that S was familiar with the Latin version of Caesar's *Commentaries,* since the immediate source of S's lines is to be found in the Golding translation.

(13)

Theobald, William, *The Classical Element in the Shakespeare Plays,* p. 122. See 9.

De bello Gallico, V, 14 influenced *2H6,* IV, vii, 65 ff.

Cardano, Girolamo

ENGLISH: *Comforte* [tr. T. Bedingfield], London, 1573.

(14)

Craig, Hardin, "Hamlet's Book," *Huntington L B,* 6 (1934): 17-37.

Although the large amount of "consolation literature" during the Renaissance prevents a categorical statement regarding S's indebtedness to this work, there are close parallels between Cardan's *De consolatione* and *H.*

Catullus, Valerius

(15)

[Cowl, R. P.] *Sources of the Text of Henry the Fourth,* Bruges, 1928, p. 43.

Carmina, XXXV, 7, of Catullus influenced *2H4,* I, i, 47 ("devour the way").

(16)

Johnstone, J. E., "The Classical Element in Shakespeare," *Catholic World,* 106 (1917): 38-52.

S's allusion to the vine's being wed to the elm in *CE,* II, ii, 178, was derived from Catullus.

(17)

McPeek, J. A. S., *Catullus in Strange and Distant Britain* (*Harvard Studies in Comparative Literature,* 15), Cambridge, 1939, *passim.*

That S shows the direct influence of Catullus cannot be proved, despite the statements to that effect by R. M. Theobald and William Theobald. [See 19.] S's writings are remarkably free from the stock Catullan phrases found in many Elizabethan sonnets. Interesting parallels to Catullus, however, are cited in over half a dozen Sn works.

(18)

Robertson, J. M., *The Baconian Heresy: A Confutation,* London, 1913, pp. 208-209, 214-215.

Some passages in *LLL, 2H4, CE, Tem,* and *H,* which have been attributed to Catullan influence, were merely Elizabethan commonplaces.

(19)

Theobald, William, *The Classical Element in the Shakespeare Plays,* pp. 127-130, 333. See 9.

Passages in *CE, Tem, MA, H8, LLL, H, 2H4,* and *TGV* are cited to demonstrate the influence of Catullus on S.

Cicero, Marcus Tullius

FRENCH: *Trois oraisons . . . pour Marcellus . . . pour . . . Pompée . . . pour Ligarius,* tr. Est. Leblanc, Paris, 1544.

ITALIAN: *Orazioni,* tr. Fausto da Longiano, Venice, 1556.

Le orazioni, tr. Lodovico Dolce, Venice, 1562.

Orazioni . . . per Q. Ligario [tr. attributed to Brunetto Latini], Lyons, 1578.

La divinazione . . . contra C. Verre, tr. M. Gio. Giustiniano, Padua, 1549.

I sette libri . . . contra Cajo Verre, tr. Gioseffo Tramezzino, Venice, 1554.

Dialogo dell' oratore, tr. L. Dolce, Venice, 1547.

SPANISH: *Las quatro oraciones contra Catilina, oraciones por la Ley Manilia, por Q. Ligario, por Marcello, y Archias Poeta,* tr. Petrus Simon Abril [no pl., n. d.].

Accusationis in C. Verrem liber, tr. Petrus Simon Abril, Saragossa, 1574.

ENGLISH: *De amicicia* [tr. J. Tiptoft, London, 1530?].

The Thre Bookes of Tullyes Offyces, tr. R. Whytinton [*sic*], London, 1534.

The Paradox, tr. R. Whittington [no pl.], 1540.

The Booke of Freendeship [tr. J. Harington], London, 1550.

Three Bookes of Dueties, tr. N. Grimalde, London, 1558. See 261.

Those Fyve Questions Which Cicero Disputed in His Manor of Tusculanum, tr. J. Dolman, London, 1561.

Principia latine loquendi scribendique sive selecta quaedam ex Ciceronis epistolis, tr. T. W., London, 1575.

"Certaine Selected Epistles out of M. T. Cicero" in *A Panoplie of Epistles* by Abraham Fleming, London, 1576.

Foure Severall Treatises: Conteyninge . . . Discourses of Frendshippe, Old Age, Paradoxes, and Scipio His Dreame, tr. T. Newton, London, 1577.

For a plagiarism of Cicero, see 56.

See also Introduction, footnote 5.

(20)

Addington, M. H., "Shakespeare and Cicero," *NQ,* 165 (1933) : 116-118.

A careful study is made of the parallels between the "To be, or not to be" soliloquy in *H,* III, i, and the first chapter of John Dolman's translation of Cicero's *Tusculan Disputations.*

(21)

C., T. C., *"Hamlet,* Three Notes," *NQ,* 175 (1938): 114.

The figure of "the mind's eye" in *H,* I, i, 112 and I, ii, 185, occurs in Cicero's *Orator,* 101. Probably, S had not read the phrase in the original, but had obtained the concept from the conversation of a friend.

(22)

Carver, P. L., "The Source of the 'Mind's Eye,' " *NQ,* 175 (1938): 191.

S need not have obtained the expression, "the mind's eye" from Cicero's second *Oration against Verres.* It is imitated in the pseudo-Latin play, *Acolastus,* which was republished as a school text with an English translation in 1540.

(23)

[Cowl, R. P.] *Sources of the Text of Henry the Fourth,* p. 42. See 15.

Cicero's *De fato,* III, was the source of *1H4,* III, i, 18 ff. ("Why, so it would have done at the same season . . .").

(24)

Hibernicus, " 'The Mind's Eye,' " *NQ*, 175 (1938) : 158-159.

Besides the Ciceronian parallel noted by T. C. C., there are two additional passages from which the concept of "the mind's eye" might have been taken: Cicero's *De natura deorum*, I, 19 or *De oratore*, III, 163. It is also to be found in the Latin (but not in the Golding) version of Ovid's *Metamorphoses*, XV, 63 and in Ovid's *Ex Ponto*, VIII, 34.

(25)

Jaggard, William, *Shakespeare Once a Printer and Bookman*, p. 11. See 2.

Cicero is referred to by name in *2H6*, IV, i, 136; *Titus*, IV, i, 14; and *JC*, *passim*.

(26)

Proestler, Mary, "Caesar Did Never Wrong but with Just Cause," *PQ*, 7 (1928) : 91-92.

JC, III, i, 47-48 ("Caesar doth not wrong, nor without cause Will he be satisfied") was possibly derived from the Euripidean fragment which, according to Cicero in *De officiis* and to Suetonius in *Lives of the Caesars*, Caesar frequently quoted. The fact that Holland did not translate *Lives of the Caesars* until 1606 militates against S's having obtained the concept from Suetonius. For Renaissance translations of the latter, see Suetonius.

(27)

Robertson, J. M., *The Baconian Heresy*, pp. 203 ff., 213 f., 242. See 18.

Some of the claims of Ciceronian influence on *H5*, *Timon*, and *TC* are refuted.

(28)

Sandys, J. E., "Scholarship" in *Shakespeare's England*, p. 268. See 12.

As has been suggested in J. M. Robertson's *Montaigne and Shakespeare*, one of the sources of *TC*, III, iii, 95-117, was Dolman's translation of Cicero's *Tusculan Disputations*. [Note: Robertson's *Montaigne and Shakespeare* was originally published before 1904 and, therefore, does not fall within the scope of this bibliography.]

(29)

Sonnenschein, E. A., "Shakspere and Stoicism," *The University R*, 1 (1905) : 23-41.

Titus, I, i, 117 ff. ("Wilt thou draw near the nature of the gods? . . .") might have been derived from *Pro Ligario*, XIII, 32.

(30)

Staedler, Erich, "Die klassischen Quellen der Antoniusrede in Shakespeares *Julius Caesar*," *Neuphilologische Monatsschrift*, 10 (1939) : 235-245.

Antony's speech, "Friends, Romans, countrymen . . ." (*JC*, III, ii, 79 ff.), shows the influence of all the classical material on the subject. In fact, much of the speech was borrowed directly from the writers of antiquity. Since S's knowledge of the classics was derived through translation, this speech was probably written by Marlowe and Beaumont, with some technical assistance from S. The influence of the following classical works is noted (line references are given) : Cicero's *Epistolae ad Atticum;* Velleius Paterculus' *Historiae Romanae;* Petronius' *Bellum civile;* Tacitus' *Annales;* Plutarch's lives of Caesar, Brutus, and Antony; Suetonius' *Vitae Caesarum;* Florus' *Epitome rerum Romanorum;* Appian's *Historia Romana;* and Cassius' *Historia Romana.*

(31)

Theobald, William, *The Classical Element in the Shakespeare Plays,* pp. 132-139. See 9.

Lines in S's works are cited which show the influence of passages in a number of Cicero's writings.

Claudianus, Claudius

FRENCH: *Le Ravisement de Proserpine,* tr. Desroches, Paris, 1586.

ITALIAN: *La rapina di Proserpina,* tr. Livio Sanuto, Venice, 1551.

Del ratto di Proserpina, tr. Annibale Nozzolini, Lucca, 1560.

[*Rape of Proserpina*] tr. Nicolo Biffi, Milan, 1584.

Il ratto di Proserpina, tr. Giovan Domenico Bevilacqua, Palermo, 1585.

Il rapimento di Proserpina, tr. M. Ant. Cinuzzi Scacciato Intronato, Venice, 1608.

SPANISH: *Robo de Proserpina* [tr. Francisco Faria], Madrid, 1608.

(32)

Hamilton, M. P., "A Latin and English Passage on Dreams," *SP*, 33 (1936) : 1-9.

The dreams mentioned in *RJ*, I, iv, 53-88, were borrowed from Claudian. A Variorum footnote on this passage is noted.

(33)

Jaggard, William, *Shakespeare Once a Printer and Bookman,* p. 11. See 2.

Although S never mentioned Claudian in his writings and although no English translation of Claudian's *Rape of Proserpina* was published before S's death, this work seems to have influenced S's *Lucrece* and may also explain the references to Proserpina in *TC*, II, i, 37 and in *WT*, IV, iii, 116.

(34)

Krappe, A. H., "Shakespeare Notes," *A*, 52 (1928) : 174-182. [*R3*, pp. 174-175.]

The passage in *De bello Gothico* beginning *"Hic celer effecit"* was the ultimate source and, perhaps, the direct source of *R3*, I, i, 1-4 ("Now is the winter of our discontent . . ."").

(35)

Theobald, William, *The Classical Element in the Shakespeare Plays*, pp. 139-142. See 9.

Passages in *1H4, 3H6, KL, LLL, Tem, Titus*, and *Mac* are cited as showing the influence of Claudian.

Colonna, Egidio *alias* Aegidius Romanus

FRENCH: *Le Mirouer . . . du regime et gouvernement des roys* [tr. Henri de Ganchy or Gauchy], Paris, 1517.

SPANISH: *Regiment* [*sic*] *dels princeps* [tr. Arnal Strayol?], Barcelona, 1480.

Regimiento de los principes [tr. Juan Garcia de Castro-Xeris], Seville, 1494.

(36)

Benham, A. R., "The Renewal of the Hundred Years' War in Shakespeare," *PQ*, 6 (1927) : 303-306.

In *H5*, I, i, the clergy hope that the continuation of the French war will distract the people from their plans to confiscate church property. This motive for the continuation of the war might have been directly suggested to S by a reading of *Liber de regimine principum*, either in the original Latin or in a continental translation.

Colonne, Guido Delle

ENGLISH: *The Auncient Historie and Onely Trewe and Syncere Cronicle of the Warres betwixte the Grecians and the Troyans . . . wrytten by*

Daretus a Troyan and Dictus a Grecian . . . digested in Latyn by . . . Guydo de Columpnis . . . , tr. [with additions] John Lydgate, London, 1555.

See also **Dictys.**

For Caxton's translation of Le Fevre's version of Colonne see under **Le Fevre.**

(37)

Henderson, W. B. D., "Shakespeare's *Troilus and Cressida* Yet Deeper in Its Tradition" in *Essays in Dramatic Literature (The Parrott Presentation Volume)*, ed. Hardin Craig, Princeton, 1935, pp. 127-156.

A detailed listing of parallels is offered to show that Lydgate's *Troy Book* was, unquestionably, one of the sources of *TC.*

(38)

Keller, Wolfgang, "Shakespeares *Troilus und Cressida*," *SJ*, 66 (1930): 182-207. [P. 191.]

Lydgate did not influence *TC.*

See also 283 and 381.

Culmann, Leonhard

Lists of S's schoolbooks generally include Culmann's *Sententiae pueriles.* See also Introduction, footnote 5.

(39)

Kröger, Ernst, *Die Sage von Macbeth bis zu Shakspere (Palaestra,* 39), Berlin, 1904, *Mac* sources: pp. 157-216, 226-229. [P. 228.]

In *Mac* II, iii, 83, the expression, "sleep, death's counterfeit," was derived from *"somnus mortis imago"* [*sic*] of *Sententiae pueriles.*

(40)

Plimpton, G. A., *The Education of Shakespeare*, London, New York, 1933, ix, 140 pp.

This book is valuable as a collection of schoolbooks available in the Sn period. Its discussions of specific Sn sources, such as *Sententiae pueriles,* is derived from H. R. D. Anders' *Shakespeare's Books.*

(41)

Sandys, J. E., "Education" in *Shakespeare's England,* Oxford, 1916, I: 224-250. [Culmann, pp. 233-234.]

"Belli incertus exitus" of *Sententiae pueriles* suggested *Cor,* V, iii, 141; *"doloris medicus tempus"* inspired *TGV,* III, ii, 15 and *Cym,* III, v, 37-38.

Du Bellay, Joachim

(42)

Ward, H. G., "Du Bellay and Shakespeare," *NQ,* 155 (1928): 417.

Du Bellay's "Petronillae puellae" probably influenced *H,* V, i, 266 ff. ("I hop'd thou shouldst have been my Hamlet's wife . . .").

Erasmus, Desiderius

ENGLISH: *Proverbes or Adagies with Newe Addicions, Gathered out of the Chiliades* by R. Taverner, London, 1539.
The Praise of Folie, tr. T. Chaloner, London, 1549.
A Dialogue of Communication of Two Persons [no tr., London, 1540?].
A Very Pleasaunt and Fruitful Diologe Called the Epicure [no tr.], London, 1545.
Two Dyaloges, tr. E. Becke, Canterbury [1550].
A Mery Dialogue, Declarynge the Propertyes of Shrowde Shrewes, and Honest Wyves, tr. Abraham Vele, London, 1557.
One Dialogue or Colloquy Entitled Diversoria, tr. E. H., London, 1566.
Seven Dialogues Both Pithie and Profitable, tr. W. B[urton], London, 1606.

See also Introduction, footnote 5.

(43)

Bush, Douglas, *Mythology and the Renaissance Tradition in English Poetry,* Minneapolis, London, 1932, p. 154.

The greater part of Lucrece's address to opportunity is to be found in the comment on *"Nosce tempus"* in Taverner's *Proverbes or Adagies Gathered out of the Chiliades of Erasmus.* (A similar apostrophe is to be found in Spenser.)

(44)

Bush, Douglas, "Notes on Shakespeare's Classical Mythology," *PQ,* 6 (1927): 295-302. [*Lucrece,* pp. 301-302.]

The same suggestion is made as in 43.

(45)

Ford, Daniel, "Shakespeare and Aristotle," *N*, 96 (1913): 34.

TC, II, ii, 165 ff. ("not much Unlike young men, whom Aristotle . . .") is a misquotation of Aristotle's *Nichomachean Ethics*. Erasmus, in his address to the reader entitled "De utilitate colloquiorum" in *Colloquia familiaria*, was responsible for the error.

(46)

Henderson, W. B. D., "Shakespeare's *Troilus and Cressida* Yet Deeper in Its Tradition," Erasmus: pp. 153-156. See 37.

Quotations are offered to support the thesis that *TC* was strongly influenced by Erasmus, especially by his *Praise of Folly*.

(47)

Hutton, James, "Honorificabilitudinitatibus," *MLN*, 46 (1931): 392-395.

Erasmus' *Adagia*, III, ii, 69 was a possible source of the word, "honorificabilitudinitatibus," *LLL*, V, i, 45. The word, however, was commonplace.

(48)

Keller, Wolfgang, "Eine neue Quelle für den *Sturm*," *SJ*, 57 (1921): 122-123.

J. D. Rea is not justified in suggesting that "Naufragium" in *Colloquia* displaces Somer's account as a source of *Tem*. See 50.

(49)

Rea, J. D., "Jaques in Praise of Folly," *MP*, 17 (1919): 465-469.

The influence of Erasmus' *Praise of Folly* may be seen in *AYL*, not only in Jaques' disquisition on fools and folly, but also in his speech on the seven ages of man and in Rosalind's complaint against Cupid, IV, i, 49 ff., as well as in various comments of Touchstone.

(50)

Rea, J. D., "A Source for the Storm in *The Tempest*," *MP*, 17 (1919): 279-286.

Erasmus' colloquy, "Naufragium," in the Burton translation, is a more probable source of the storm in *Tem* than is the account in Jourdain's pamphlet. Extracts from the Burton translation are quoted to demonstrate the similarities in the characters, the setting, and in the description of St. Elmo's fire. See 48.

(51)

Theobald, William, *The Classical Element in the Shakespeare Plays*, pp.
  152-155. See 9.

The influence of Erasmus' *Christiani matrimonii institutio, Adagia,* and
Colloquia on specific passages in S is noted.

See also 111, 167, 262, 263, and 464.

Florus, Lucius Annaeus

ENGLISH: *The Romane Historie* [of Titus Livius] : *Also the Breviaries of L.
Florus,* tr. P. Holland, London, 1600.

See also **Livy.**

(52)

Theobald, William, *The Classical Element in the Shakespeare Plays*, p. 165.
  See 9.

AC, II, v, 33 ff. ("bring it to that . . .") was derived from Florus, II, ii.

See also 30.

Gallus, Cornelius

(53)

Noble, Richmond, *Shakespeare's Use of Song with the Text of the Principal Songs,* Oxford, 1923, p. 90.

Ad Lydiam, ascribed to Gallus, was the source of *MM,* IV, i, 1 ff. ("Take,
O take those lips away . . .").

"Gesta Romanorum"

ENGLISH: *Gesta Romanorum* [no tr. (almost identical with the tr. in MS
Harleian, 7333)], London [1510-1515?].

Gesta Romanorum [revised by Richard Robinson], London, 1577.

Gesta Romanorum is sometimes included in lists of *MV* sources. Usually,
  however, it is mentioned merely as an ultimate, rather than as a direct,
  source.

(54)

Brown, B. D., "Exemplum Materials Underlying *Macbeth*," *PMLA*, 50 (1935) : 700-714.

Although echoes of *Gesta Romanorum* are to be found in *Mac*, these are to be explained as the result of oral, rather than written, tradition.

(55)

Lawrence, W. W., *Shakespeare's Problem Comedies*, New York, 1931, p. 20.

It is uncertain from what source S obtained the casket theme of *MV*. It might have been obtained from Richard Robinson's edition of *Gesta Romanorum*, 1577.

See also 146 and 473.

Goslicius, Laurentius Grimaldus

ENGLISH: *The Counsellor Exactly Pourtraited in Two Bookes* [no tr.], London, 1598.

(56)

Brückner, A., "Zum Namen Polonius," *Ar*, 132 (1914) : 404-405.

Roman Dybowski, in his introduction to a Polish edition of *H*, denies that there is any connection between Polonius and Goslicius. I. Gollancz has suggested that Goslicius' *De optimo senatore* was one of S's sources. [See 57 and 58.] It was available to S in the translation of 1598 and was a plagiarism of Cicero.

(57)

Gollancz, I., "Bits of Timber" in *A Book of Homage to Shakespeare*, ed. Israel Gollancz, Oxford, 1916, pp. 172-177.

Not only did S derive the name of Polonius from Goslicius, but from that source he also obtained some of the loftiest sentiments of *H* and, perhaps, ideas for the characterization of Angelo in *MM*. See 56.

(58)

Gollancz, I., "The Name Polonius," *Ar*, 132 (1914) : 141-144.

S changed the name Corambus to Polonius in order to show that he was alluding not to Burleigh but to the Pole, Goslicius, author of *De optimo sena-*

tore. Passages are cited to show the influence of this work on *MM* and *H*. See 56.

Grimaldus, see Goslicius

Horatius Flaccus, Quintus

FRENCH: *Les Œuvres,* tr. M. Luc de la Porte *et al.,* Paris, 1584.
Les Œuvres, tr. Robert et Anthoine le Chevalier d'Agneaux, Paris, 1588.
Les Cinq Livres des odes, tr. J[acques] Mondot, Paris, 1579.
[3 odes] tr. Jacques Peletier in his *Œuvres poetiques,* Paris, 1547.

ITALIAN: *I Cinque libri dell' odi,* tr. G. Giorgini, Jesi, 1595.
Odi diverse, tr. Giov. Narducci da Perugia, Venice, 1605.

SPANISH: *Sus obras,* tr. [Juan] Villen de Biedma, Granada, 1599.
Arte poética y algunas odas [no tr.], Madrid, 1591.

ENGLISH: *A Medicinable Morall, That Is the Two Bookes of Horace His Satyres Englyshed. . . . Also Epigrammes,* tr. T. Drant, London, 1566.
Horace His Art of Poetrie, Pistles and Satyrs, tr. Th. Drant, London, 1567.
See also Introduction, footnote 5.

(59)

Blunden, Edmund, "The Madness of Lear," *N and Athenaeum,* 43 (1928) : 458-459.

Horace's *Epistles,* II, i, 210-214 were echoed by Lear when Edgar entered as a madman. The last ode of the first book of Horace's *Odes* suggested Lear's jest on Edgar's "Persian" attire.

(60)

Blunden, Edmund, *Shakespeare's Significances (Shakespeare Association Papers,* 15), London, 1928, pp. 7-9. [Reprinted in Edmund Blunden, *The Mind's Eye,* London, 1934, pp. 201-203.]

Reminiscences of Horace were interwoven into the mad speeches of King Lear.

(61)

Brandl, Alois, *Shakespeare,* Berlin, 1922, p. 30.

The description of the Roman's joy regarding Pompey, described in *JC,* I, i, 40 ff., was dependent on Horace's *Carmina,* I, xx, 5.

(62)

[Cowl, R. P.] *Sources of the Text of Henry the Fourth,* p. 42. See 15.

Horace's *Carmina,* IV, ii, 26 might have suggested the "fiery Pegasus" of *1H4,* IV, i, 109.

(63)

Gilbert, A. H., "Falstaff's Impresa," *NQ,* 164 (1933) : 389.

2H4, IV, iii, 56 ("I in the clear sky of fame . . .") and Horace's *Odes,* I, xii, 46-49 are similar. S might have found the concept in a text of Horace or in a collection of *imprese.*

(64)

Greenwood, G. G., *Is There a Shakespeare Problem?* London, New York, 1916, pp. 127-129.

The fifty-fifth sonnet of S was based on Horace's *Odes,* III, xxx.

(65)

Greenwood, G. G., *The Shakespeare Problem Restated,* New York, London, 1908, p. 92 n.

The same suggestion is made as in 64.

(66)

Haines, C. R., *The Carmina of Quintus Horatius Flaccus (Together with Satire I, lx) Rendered into English Rhyming Verse and Accompanied by the Latin Text,* London [1933], pp. iii, v-viii.

John Churton Collins and the Baconians have exaggerated the extent of S's knowledge of the classics. However, although certain of their suggestions regarding S's dependence upon Horace should be discounted, there remain passages in about half of S's plays which demonstrate the actual influence of Horace upon S. These are cited.

(67)

Jaggard, William, *Shakespeare Once a Printer and Bookman,* p. 15. See 2.

Horace is named in *LLL,* IV, ii, 105 and in *Titus,* IV, ii, 22, 24.

(68)

Johnstone, J. E., "The Classical Element in Shakespeare." See 16.

Polonius' remark: "Though this be madness, yet there is method in't" (*H,* II, ii, 211-212) was derived from Horace's *Satires,* II, iii, 271: *"Insanire paret certa ratione modoque."* Horatian influence may also be found in S's sonnets.

(69)

Lathrop, H. B., *Translations from the Classics into English from Caxton to Chapman, 1447-1620 (U of Wisconsin Studies in Language and Literature,* 35), Madison, 1933, p. 146.

The reference to a stepmother's unkindness in the opening of *MND* is too familiar a concept to be used as evidence that S was familiar with Drant's translation of Horace's *Epistles,* I, i, 20 ff.

(70)

Mangold, W., "Zu *Hamlet,* II, 2, 321," *SJ,* 44 (1908): 146-147.

A possible source of *H,* II, ii, 329-330 ("man delights not me; no, nor woman neither") was Horace's *Carmina,* IV, iv, 29.

(71)

Robertson, J. M., *The Baconian Heresy, passim.* See 18.

S's familiarity with Horace is proved neither by his use of two well-known Latin quotations, nor by his reference to a "method in madness" which could have been obtained from a translation of the *Satires.* A number of so-called borrowings from Horace in about a half dozen Sn plays were, actually, derived from proverbial expressions or from contemporary English drama.

(72)

Stronach, George, "Shakespeare's Scholarship," *NQ,* Tenth Series, 1 (1904): 33-34.

John Churton Collins is correct in suggesting Horatian influence in *R3, MA, MV.* [Note: Since Collins' articles on S's classical background first appeared in 1903, they do not fall within the scope of this study.]

(73)

Theobald, William, *The Classical Element in the Shakespeare Plays,* pp. 209-223. See 9.

There is a detailed listing of S's specific borrowings from Horace.

Hrotsvita

(74)

Stewart, H. H., "Romeo's First Love," *Baconiana,* Third Series, 9 (1911): 191-197.

When writing *H5* and *MM*, S had in mind the Latin plays of the tenth century nun, Hrotsvita. The most striking resemblance to the nun's plays, however, is to be found in *RJ*, I, i. The parallels are discussed in detail.

Juvenalis, Decius Junius

FRENCH: *Quatre satyres*, tr. Michel d'Amboyse, Paris, 1544.

ITALIAN: *Satirae italice*, tr. Georgio Summaripa, Treviso, 1480.

SPANISH: *Satira dezena*, tr. Pero Fernandez [or Jeronimo] de Villegas, Burgos, 1519.

See also Introduction, footnote 5.

(75)

Johnstone, J. E., "The Classical Element in Shakespeare." See 16.

The eighth satire of Juvenal or a passage in Euripides was the source of *MV*, I, i, 83 ("Why should a man, whose blood is warm within . . .").

(76)

Smart, J. S., *Shakespeare: Truth and Tradition*, with a Memoir by W. Macneile Dixon, London, 1928, p. 163.

When asked by Polonius what book he had in his hand (*H*, II, ii, 195 ff.), Hamlet was reading the tenth satire of Juvenal.

(77)

Stronach, George, "Shakespeare's Scholarship." See 72.

H, KL, AC, Cym, and *1H4* were strongly influenced by Juvenal.

(78)

Review: Theobald, W., "Shakespeare's Books," *Baconiana*, Third Series, 3 (1905) : 27-35.

In his dissertation, *Shakespeare's Books*, H. R. D. Anders does not do justice to S's use of Juvenal. Theobald cites twenty-six parallels to Juvenal in over a dozen Sn plays.

(79)

Theobald, William, *The Classical Element in the Shakespeare Plays*, pp. 227-235. See 9.

Over a score of passages in S's plays show some similarity to Juvenal. Some of these passages, however, might have been derived from other sources.

Livius, Titus

ENGLISH: *The Romane Historie* [of Livy]: *Also the Breviaries of L. Florus*, tr. P. Holland, London, 1600.

William Painter, *The Palace of Pleasure*, London, 1566, I, 1-4; II, 6, 8.

The Historie of Two the Moste Noble Captaines of the Worlde, Anniball and Scipio . . . Translated into Englishe out of the Titus Livius and Other Authoures by A[ntony] C[ope], London, 1544.

See also **Florus** and **Busche.**

See also Introduction, footnote 5.

(80)

Theobald, William, *The Classical Element in the Shakespeare Plays*, pp. 236-237. See 9.

Passages in *Mac, Titus,* and *1H6* are cited as having been dependent upon Livy.

For the influence of Livy on *Lucrece,* see 95 and 97.

Lucanus, Marcus Annaeus

FRENCH: *Lucan, Suétone et Saluste* [no tr.], Paris, 1490.

ITALIAN: *Delle guerre civili,* tr. G. Morigi, Ravenna, 1587.

Pharsalia, tr. L. Cardin de Montichiello, Milan, 1492.

SPANISH: *La historia,* tr. Mn. Lasso de Oropesa, Lisbon, 1541.

ENGLISH: *Lucans First Booke,* tr. C. Marlow, London, 1600.

(81)

Conley, C. H., "An Instance of the Fifteen Signs of Judgment in Shakespeare," *MLN*, 30 (1915): 41-44.

The portents found in *H*, I, i, 115-120 and in *JC*, II, ii, 17-24, were derived neither from Lucan's *Pharsalia* nor from Holinshed's *Chronicle*. They were derived from an Anglo-Norman version of the *Fifteen Signs of Judgment*, translated into middle English by the author of *Cursor mundi*.

(82)

Jaggard, William, *Shakespeare Once a Printer and Bookman*, p. 17. See 2.

In *O*, I, iii, 44, there is a reference to Marcus Luccicos, which was, perhaps, an adaptation of Lucan's name. The reference to Pharsalia in *AC*, III, vii, 31, might have been the result of S's acquaintance with Lucan's work on the subject.

(83)

Round, P. Z., "A Classical Quotation in *Henry VI*," *TLS*, June 14, 1928, p. 450.

2H6, IV, i, 117 *("Gelidus timor occupat artus")* was derived from Lucan's *Pharsalia*, I, 244-246 *("gelidus pavor occupat artus . . .")*. See 110.

(84)

Theobald, William, *The Classical Element in the Shakespeare Plays*, pp. 237-241. See 9.

Resemblances are cited between Lucan's writings and passages in a number of S's plays.

See also 110 and 168.

Lucretius Carus, Titus

ITALIAN: *Breve spositione di tutta l'opera di Lucretio* by Girolamo Frachetta, Venice, 1589.

(85)

Blunden, Edmund, *Shakespeare's Significances*, p. 15. [Reprinted in Edmund Blunden, *The Mind's Eye*, p. 212.] See 60.

King Lear's reference to "the mystery of things" (*KL*, V, iii, 16) might have been intended as an allusion to the title of Lucretius' poem.

(86)

Johnstone, J. E., "The Classical Element in Shakespeare." See 16.

The concept in *TC*, IV, ii, 110 ff. ("love Is as the very centre of the earth . . .") was derived from either Bacon or Lucretius. S's allusions to the combat between Hercules and the Nemean lion (*LLL*, IV, i, 90 and *H*, I, iv, 83) were derived from Hesiod, Lucretius, or Theocritus, none of which were available in English translation. The influence of Lucretius on S's sonnets is noted in passing.

(87)

Krappe, A. H., "Shakespeare Notes." See 34.

Lucretius' *De rerum natura*, V, 1151 *("inde metus maculat . . .")* suggested to S the idea of portraying Lady Macbeth's guilty conscience by having her walk and talk in her sleep.

(88)

Theobald, William, *The Classical Element in the Shakespeare Plays*, pp. 243-251. See 9.

Over a dozen Sn passages are cited which might have been influenced by Lucretius.

Mantuanus, see **Baptista Mantuanus**

Ovidius Naso, Publius

ITALIAN: *I fasti,* tr. V. Cartari, Venice, 1551.

ENGLISH: [*Amores*] *All of Ovids Elegies,* tr. C. Marlow, Middleburg [1598?].
The Flores of Ovide de arte amandi [no tr.], London, 1513.
De arte amandi or *The Art of Love* [no tr., Middleburg? 1600?].
The Heroycall Epistles, tr. G. Turbervile, London, 1567.
Ovid His Invective against Ibis [tr. T. Underdown], London, 1569.
The XV Bookes of . . . Metamorphosis, tr. A. Golding, London, 1567. [Frequently reprinted.]
The Fable of Ovid Treting of Narcissus [tr. Thomas Howell], London, 1560.
The Pleasant Fable of Hermaphroditus and Salmacis, tr. T. Peend, London, 1565.
See 120 for another English version of *The Metamorphoses.*
Ovidius Naso His Remedie of Love [tr. F. L.], London, 1600.
The Thre First Bokes of Ovids de Tristibus, tr. T. Churchyarde, London [1572].

See also Introduction, footnote 5.

Amores and *Ars Amatoria*

Surveys of S's sources frequently note that the Latin couplet on the title page of *VA* was derived from *Amores*, I, xv, 35-36; many suggest that *RJ*, II, ii, 92-93 ("at lovers' perjuries, They say, Jove laughs") was inspired by *Ars amatoria*, 633.

(89)

Clark, A. M., "A Marlowe Mystification," *TLS*, July 16, 1925, p. 480.

The opinion expressed by J. M. Robertson [see 91] is correct. It might have been Heywood who made the translation of Ovid's *Art of Love* from which *RJ*, II, ii, 92-93 was obtained.

(90)

Robertson, J. M., *The Baconian Heresy*, pp. 212, 246-247. See 18.

The concept to be found in *RJ*, II, ii, 92-93 ("at lovers' perjuries, They say, Jove laughs") is to be found not only in Ovid and Tibullus, but also in Marlowe, Greene, and Lyly. *MA*, I, i, 271 ("In time the savage bull . . .") was not derived from the *Art of Love* either; this idea is expressed in Kyd's *Spanish Tragedy* and Watson's *Hecatompathia* as well as elsewhere.

(91)

Robertson, J. M., "A Marlowe Mystification," *TLS*, December 11, 1924, p. 850.

Francis Douce erred in stating that *RJ*, II, ii, 92-93 was derived from a Marlovian translation of Ovid's *Art of Love*. Marlowe did not translate this work nor is the couplet to be found elsewhere in Marlowe's writings. See 89.

(92)

Theobald, R. M., "Ovid cum Shakespeare, cum Marlowe cum Ben Jonson," *Baconiana*, Third Series, 5 (1907): 20-24.

In an attempt to prove that Marlowe and Shakespeare's works were written by Bacon, verbal parallels are cited between Ovid's *Amores* in the Marlowe translation and passages in several Sn plays.

See also 118, 122, 124, 126, 128, 135, and 136.

Epistulae Ex Ponto

(93)

Hill, N. W., "Ovid and Shakespeare," *NQ*, Tenth Series, 8 (1907): 505.

Either Ovid or Seneca seems a more probable source of Portia's speech on mercy (*MV*, IV, i, 184 ff.) than Polynice's appeal for mercy in the *Œdipus Coloneus*, II, 267-269.

(94)

Luce, Morton, "Ovid and Shakespeare," *NQ*, Tenth Series, 7 (1907): 301.

Portia's speech on mercy (*MV*, IV, i, 184 ff.) bears an even more striking resemblance to Ovid's *Pontic Epistles*, II, ix, 11 ff., than to Seneca.

See also 24, 116, 135, and 136.

Fasti

(95)

Bush, Douglas, *Mythology and the Renaissance Tradition in English Poetry*, pp. 149-155. See 43.

S obtained the main story of Lucrece from the first book of Livy, to which he added some details from Chaucer's tale of Lucrece in *The Legende of Good Women* and from Ovid's *Fasti*. S read both Ovid's and Livy's versions of Lucrece in Latin. With the exception of one phrase, there is no evidence of S's having used Painter's translation of Livy.

(96)

Luce, Morton, "Ovid and Shakespeare." See 94.

The meaning of *Tem*, III, i, 14-15 ("But these sweet thoughts . . .") may be clarified if it is compared with *Fasti*, IV, 434.

(97)

Marschall, Wilhelm, "Das 'Argument' zu Shakespeares *Lucrece*," *A*, 53 (1929): 102-122.

S must have reread Ovid's *Fasti* before he wrote *Lucrece*. S's use of *Fasti*, and of Bandello s and Livy's versions of the Lucrece tale are analyzed in detail. See 431.

(98)

Robertson, J. M., *The Baconian Heresy*, p. 195. See 18.

S's *Lucrece* might have been influenced by a translation of *Fasti*.

See also 115, 116, 122, 124, 135, and 136.

Heroides

(99)

Boas, F. S., ed., *The Heroycall Epistles of the Learned Poet Publius Ovidius Naso, Translated into English Verse by George Turbervile, 1567*, London, 1928, p. xxii.

The dialogue of Lorenzo and Jessica in the garden at Belmont, *MV*, V, i, 1 ff., might have been influenced by Turbervile's translation of Ovid's *Heroides.*

(100)

Zielinski, Th., "Ovid und Shakespeare," *Philologus,* N. F. 18 (1905) : 17-20.

The scene of leave taking in *AC,* I, iii, was suggested not by Vergil's *Aeneid* but by the Dido epistle in Ovid's *Heroides.*

See also 104, 124, 126, 130, 135, and 136.

Ibis

See 135 and 136.

Metamorphoses

(101)

Blake, H. M., *Classic Myth in the Poetic Drama of the Age of Elizabeth,* Lancaster, Pa. [1912], pp. 23-24, 62.

S's allusions, in several plays, to the myth of Phaethon and to the chariot of the sun suggest the influence of *Metamorphoses,* II. S was familiar both with the original Latin and with the Golding translation of this work.

(102)

Brewer, Wilmon, *Ovid's Metamorphoses in European Culture (Published Together with Ovid's Metamorphoses Books I—V in English Blank Verse* by Brookes Moore)*, Boston, 1933, pp. 32-34.

S was most strongly attracted to Ovid in his earliest writings. In the period of his romantic comedies and later tragedies he became conscious of the absurdity of Ovidian mythology. His tragedies were not very much influenced by Ovid. In the period of his pastoral romances, S again resorted to mythology, but rarely of an Ovidian type.

(103)

Bush, Douglas, *Mythology and the Renaissance Tradition, VA:* pp. 139-149; *MND:* pp. 110-111. See 43.

S's borrowings in *VA* from Ovid's *Metamorphoses* and from other sources are carefully analyzed, although it is stressed that a mere listing of the Ovidian borrowings greatly exaggerates S's indebtedness to this source.

In *MND*, II, i, 109-110 ("And on old Hiems' thin and icy crown . . .") S adapted *Metamorphoses*, II, 23 ff. *("Et glacialis hiems . . .")* in an un-Ovidian manner.

(104)

[Cowl, R. P.]*Sources of the Text of Henry the Fourth, passim.* See 15.

Passages in *Metamorphoses* and *Heroides* are cited as the sources of lines in *1* and *2H4.*

(105)

Creizenach, W., "Shakespeare und Ovid," *SJ,* 41 (1905): 211.

TGV, II, vii, 25 ("The current that with gentle murmur glides . . .") was derived from *Metamorphoses,* III, 568 ff.

(106)

Creizenach, Wilhelm, *The English Drama in the Age of Shakespeare,* tr. Cécile Hugon, Philadelphia, London, 1916, pp. 74 n, 75.

The same suggestion is made as in 105. The dying Rutland's quotation from Ovid, *3H6,* I, iii, 48 *("Dii faciant . . .")* is also noted.

(107)

Dickins, Bruce, "Two Queries on *Twelfth Night,*" *MLR,* 29 (1934): 67.

Feste's jests, which Sir Andrew Aguecheek attempts to recall (*TN,* II, iii, 23 ff.), might have been based upon Ovid's *Metamorphoses,* X, 243 ff., where Pygmalion is called *"Paphius heros."* This was linked by Sir Andrew with an astrological reference to the Paphian (Venus) and the sun.

(108)

Farrand, M. L., "An Additional Source for *A Midsummer-Night's Dream,*" *SP,* 27 (1930): 233-243.

Thomas Moffett's *The Silkewormes and Their Flies* is preferred to Golding's Ovid as a source of *MND.*

(109)

Forrest, H. T. S., *The Original Venus and Adonis,* London, 1930, *passim.*

The influence of Ovid on *VA* is analyzed in order to bolster the theory that this poem was not written by the author of the S plays.

(110)

Fripp, E. I., "A Classical Quotation in *II. Henry VI,*" *TLS,* June 21, 1928,
 p. 468.

2H6, IV, i, 117 *("Gelidus timor occupat artus")* is a quotation from the
Latin of neither Lucan nor Vergil, but rather a misquotation of *Metamorphoses,* III, 40. See 83.

(111)

Fripp, E. I., "Elizabethan Proverbs," *TLS,* March 17, 1927, p. 194.

Erasmus, Lyly, and S derived their idea of the chameleon from *Metamorphoses,* XV, 411 ff. *(TGV,* II, i, 181 and II, iv, 26; *3H6,* III, ii, 191; and *H,*
III, ii, 98.)

(112)

Fripp, E. I. ,"Shakespeare: Boy and Man," *The Shakespeare R,* 1 **(1928)** :
 239-248.

S's use of Ovid in the original, especially in *H8,* is considered.

(113)

Fripp, Edgar, *Shakespeare Studies, Biographical and Literary,* London,
 1930, pp. 98-128.

S read Ovid in the original rather than in the Golding translation. Mytho-
logical elements which S derived from Ovid are listed in some detail.

(114)

Gray, Arthur, *"The Comedy of Errors,"* *TLS,* February 17, 1927, p. 108.

The name Aegeon in *CE* was derived from *Metamorphoses,* II, 10.

(115)

Greenwood, G. G., *Is There a Shakespeare Problem?* pp. 148-151. See 64.

S depended upon the original Latin of Ovid's *Metamorphoses* in *Tem* and
of *Fasti* in *Lucrece.*

(116)

Greenwood, G. G., *The Shakespeare Problem Restated,* pp. 88-92. See 65.

Passages are cited to demonstrate S's dependence upon the original Latin
versions of *Fasti, Metamorphoses,* and *Pontic Epistles.*

(117)

Haynes, French, "Shakespeare and the Troy Story," *Howard College B*

(Studies in History and Literature), 80 (1922) : 67-131. [Sources, pp. 126-131.]

The influence of the *Metamorphoses* on various Sn plays is dealt with *passim*. The influence of *Metamorphoses* on *TC* is analyzed in detail.

(118)

Jaggard, William, *Shakespeare Once a Printer and Bookman*, p. 18. See 2.

Ovid is named in *AYL*, III, iii, 8; *LLL*, IV, ii, 127-128; and *TS*, I, i, 33. His *Metamorphoses* is mentioned in *Titus*, IV, i, 14; and his *Art of Love* in *TS*, IV, ii, 8.

(119)

Keller, Wolfgang, "Shakespeares *Troilus und Cressida*." See 38.

S's characterizations of Agamemnon and Nestor were not intended as satirical portraits of contemporaries, nor were they based upon the Homeric interpretation. Both they and Ulysses show the influence of *Metamorphoses*, XIII.

(120)

Koeppel, E., "Randglossen zu dem Andersschen Werk über Shakespeares Belesenheit," *Ar*, 113 (1904) : 49-55. [P. 49.]

Among the versions of *Metamorphoses* which S might have used, one should consider Abraham Fraunce's *Third Part of the Countesse of Pembrokes Yvychurch*, 1592.

(121)

Kröger, Ernst, *Die Sage von Macbeth bis zu Shakspere*, pp. 227-228. See 39.

Mac, IV, i was based on *Metamorphoses*, VII, 262 ff. The figure of "Pale Hecate" in *Mac*, II, i, 52, was derived from either Ovid or Seneca.

(122)

Lee, Sidney, "Ovid and Shakespeare's Sonnets," *The Quarterly R*, 210 (1909) : 455-476.

S was familiar both with the original Latin and with the Golding translation of *Metamorphoses*. The dependence of S's plays and poems on *Metamorphoses*, *Fasti*, and *Amores* is illustrated by a fairly detailed list of borrowings.

(123)

Liebermann, F., "Shakespeare als Bearbeiter des *King John*," *Ar*, 142 (1921) : 177-202. [P. 179 n.]

Ovid's description of chaos *(Metamorphoses,* I) might have suggested to S the word, "indigest," which he used in *KJ,* V, vii, 26.

(124)

Owen, S. G., "Ovid and Romance" in *English Literature and the Classics,* lectures collected by G. S. Gordon, Oxford, 1912, pp. 167-195. [S, pp. 185-190.]

Passages from a number of Sn works are cited to show the extent of S's borrowings from *Metamorphoses, Ars amatoria, Heroides, Tristia,* and the Latin of *Fasti.*

(125)

Ready, E. P., *A Discussion of the Sources of Shakespeare's A Midsummer Night's Dream,* MS Thesis, CL, 1914, *passim.*

S's immediate source of the Pyramus and Thisbe interlude in *MND* was Ovid. Chaucer and Boccaccio are considered, but discarded, as possible sources.

(126)

Rick, Leo, "Shakespeare und Ovid," *SJ,* 55 (1919) : 35-53.

Parallels to Ovid in over twenty-five Sn plays are listed, although it is admitted that some of these similarities might have been the result of coincidence rather than of borrowing. The only definite basis for suggesting S's use of the *Metamorphoses* in the Golding translation is to be found in *Tem.* No passage in S offers positive proof of his having employed a translation, rather than the original, of *Heroides, Tristia, Amores, Ars,* or *Remedia.*

(127)

Rouse, W. H. D., ed., *Shakespeare's Ovid, Being Arthur Golding's Translation of the Metamorphoses,* London, 1904, 322 pp.

Some of S's borrowings from Ovid are noted. The source discussion, however, is not original, but is based upon H. R. D. Anders' *Shakespeare's Books.* See 132.

(128)

Sandys, J. E., "Education" and "Scholarship" in *Shakespeare's England,* pp. 235, 261-263. See 12 and 41.

Passages from *Tem, O, VA, MND, LLL, MV, Cym,* and *Titus* are cited to show the influence of Ovid on S. S was probably not at school when he learned the passage of *Ars amatoria* which influenced *RJ,* II, ii, 92-93, "At lovers' perjuries. . . ." See 237.

(129)

Schaubert, Else v., "Die Stelle vom 'rauhen Pyrrhus' (*Hamlet* II, 2, 460-551) in ihrem Verhältnis zu Marlowe-Nashes *Dido*, zu Seneca und dem *Ur-Hamlet* . . .," *A*, 53 (1929) : 374-439.

Although A. C. Bradley in *Shakespearean Tragedy* suggests that the "hounds of Sparta" in *MND*, IV, i, 120, was suggested by Seneca, the Arden edition of S suggests Ovid's *Metamorphoses* as the source.

(130)

Sedgwick, W. B., "The Influence of Ovid," *19 C*, 122 (1937) : 483-494. [S, pp. 489-491.]

The passage on Dido in *MV*, V, i, 9 ff. ("In such a night . . .") was, probably, not inspired by Vergil. It is reminiscent of the Ovidian concept, found in *Heroides*, of Dido's sending a final despairing letter, before determining on death. Lorenzo's other classical allusions in this passage were all based on Ovid, the only classical poet to exert an important influence on S, especially on his early work. This influence was, probably, largely exerted through the Golding translation.

(131)

Shackford, M. H., "*Julius Caesar* and Ovid," *MLN*, 41 (1926) : 172-174.

In *JC*, S used Ovid's *Metamorphoses*, XV, to supplement the portents described by Plutarch in his "Life of Caesar." The problem is considered in some detail, over a dozen passages from *JC* being quoted.

(132)

Review: "*Shakespeare's Ovid* . . . edited by W. H. D. Rouse . . . ," *Athenaeum*, November 5, 1904, pp. 617-618.

W. H. D. Rouse does not stress sufficiently S's dependence on Ovid. This may be explained by the fact that the Ovidian material which S used had long been in his consciousness and had been completely assimilated. See 127.

(133)

Sheppard, J. T., *Aeschylus and Sophocles: Their Work and Influence*, New York, 1927, pp. 134-135.

S did not obtain all of his Ovid through Golding's translation. It was from the original Latin that he obtained, for example, Hecate's "vaporous drop" (*Mac*, III, v, 24) on the corner of the moon.

(134)

Spencer, Hazelton, "Shakespeare's Use of Golding in *Venus and Adonis*," *MLN*, 44 (1929) : 435-437.

S did not obtain very much material for *VA* from Ovid's *Metamorphoses*. The Ovidian echoes that can be found in this poem, however, must be attributed to the influence of Golding's translation.

(135)

Theobald, W., *"Shakespeare's Books."* See 78.

S's classical attainments are not stressed sufficiently in H. R. D. Anders' *Shakespeare's Books*. Over seventy Sn passages were influenced by the various books of Ovid's *Metamorphoses*. At least twenty-four Sn passages were derived from *Amores, Ars amatoria, Epistulae, Fasti, Heroides, Ibis,* and *Tristia*.

(136)

Theobald, William, *The Classical Element in the Shakespeare Plays*, pp. 262-277. See 9.

Sn passages are listed which show the influence of Ovid's *Metamorphoses, Amores, Ars amatoria, Epistulae, Fasti, Heroides, Ibis,* and *Tristia*.

(137)

Yardley, E., *"Henry VI, Part II*, IV, i," *NQ*, Tenth Series, 6 (1906) : 324.

The Latin quotation in *2H6*, IV, i, 117 *("Gelidus timor . . .")* fuses Ovid's *Metamorphoses*, III, ii, 39-40, 47, and 100.

See also 24, 167, and 317.

Pontic Epistles, see *Epistulae Ex Ponto*

Remedia Amoris

See 126.

Tristia

See 124, 126, 135, and 136.

Paterculus, see **Velleius Paterculus**

Petronius, Gaius

(138)

Theobald, William, *The Classical Element in the Shakespeare Plays*, pp. 288-291. See 9.

Passages in *1H4, 1H6, MND, JC, RJ*, and *O* show the influence of Petronius' *Satires*. A passage in *RJ* was influenced by the *Fragmenta*.

See also 30.

Plautus, Titus Maccius

ITALIAN: *l'Amphitriona*, tr. Pandolfo Colonutio, Venice, 1530.
Cassina, tr. Gerol. Berrardo [*sic*], Venice, 1530.
Menechmi, tr. G. Berardo, Venice, 1530.
Mustellaria, tr. Geronimo Berardo, Venice, 1530.
SPANISH: *O comedia de Amphitrion* [tr. Fernan Perez de Oliva, no pl., 1525?].
Amphytrion, tr. Francisco Lopez de Villalobos, Zamora, 1517.
La comedia . . . intitulada Menechmos [no tr.], Antwerp, 1555.
La comedia . . . intitulada Milite glorioso [no tr.], Antwerp, 1555.
GERMAN: *Amphitruo*, tr. Wolfhart Spangenberg, Strassburg, 1608.
Die comedia . . . in Menechino genannt, tr. Albrecht von Eybe [no pl.], 1511.
ENGLISH: *Menaecmi*, tr. W. W[arner], London, 1595.

See also Introduction, footnote 5.

INFLUENCE OF PLAUTUS ON *CE*

(139)

Alexander, Peter, *Shakespeare's Henry VI and Richard III (Shakespeare's Problems)*, Cambridge, 1929, pp. 139-140.

That S could read Plautus in the original is demonstrated by the fact that in *CE* he was dependent not only on *Menaechmi* but also on *Amphitruo*, and in *TS* on *Mostellaria*.

(140)

Benham, A. R., "A Note on *The Comedy of Errors*," *MLN*, 36 (1921): 377-378.

Perhaps S obtained a hint for the pathos of Aegeon's plight from lines 34-36 of the prose prologue of *Menaechmi*.

(141)

Charlton, H. B., "Shakespeare's Recoil from Romanticism," *John Rylands L B*, 15 (1931) : 35-59. [Also reprinted as a separate work.]

An analysis of the characteristics of Roman comedy is followed by a detailed comparison of the Plautine and Sn versions of *CE*. Stress is laid on the romantic quality of S's play and on its transformation of the classical characters.

(142)

Connely, Willard, "When Plautus Is Greater Than Shakspere (Imprints of *Menaechmi* on *Comedy of Errors*)," *Classical J*, 19 (1924) : 303-305.

CE is a poor imitation of *Menaechmi*. See 160.

(143)

Coulter, C. C., "The Plautine Tradition in Shakespeare," *J of English and Germanic Philology*, 19 (1920) : 66-83.

The influence of classical comedy on Sn dramatic structure, plot, and dialogue is analyzed. Direct borrowings from Plautus are not stressed, although they are alluded to *passim*.

(144)

Enk, P. J., "Shakespeare's 'Small Latin,' " *Neophilologus*, 5 (1920) : 359-365.

Passages from a number of Sn plays are quoted to show S's dependence on Plautus' *Captivi, Rudens,* and *Amphitruo.* Although one may assume lost translations of these works, it is more probable that S read them and *Menaechmi* in the original. See 205.

(145)

Gaw, Allison, "Evolution of *The Comedy of Errors*," *PMLA*, 41 (1926) : 620-666. [Especially pp. 624-630.]

Menaechmi and *Amphitruo* were skillfully blended into a pre-Sn play upon which *CE* was based. The Plautine elements retained in this English version are noted in detail.

(146)

Gill, E. M., "The Plot-Structure of *The Comedy of Errors* in Relation to its Source," *Studies in English*, No. 10 (*U of Texas B*, No. 3026), 1930, pp. 13-65.

A tabulated analysis, scene by scene, of S's plot elements and of their sources demonstrates that *CE* was based upon the Latin versions of *Menaechmi* and *Amphitruo,* with some additional details from the story of Apollonius of Tyre in *Gesta Romanorum.*

(147)

Gill, Erma, "A Comparison of the Characters in *The Comedy of Errors* with Those in the *Menaechmi,*" *Studies in English,* No. 5 (*U of Texas B,* No. 2538), 1925, pp. 79-95.

The characteristics of the *dramatis personae* in *Menaechmi* and in *CE* are tabulated in order to demonstrate the superiority of the Sn version.

(148)

Gray, Arthur, "*The Comedy of Errors.*" See 114.

S misunderstood, either in the Latin or in W. W.'s English translation, *Menaechmi,* 236. This error in the interpretation of "*Graeca exotica*" in *CE,* I, i, 132, may be explained by S's use of Cooper's *Thesaurus,* the standard Latin dictionary of the time.

(149)

Greenwood, G. G., *Is There a Shakespeare Problem?* pp. 136-142. See 64.

Arguments of J. C. Collins [see 72 n.] are repeated in order to substantiate the claim that *CE* was dependent on the original of Plautus rather than on some English version of the story.

(150)

Greenwood, G. G., *The Shakespeare Problem Restated,* pp. 92-93. See 65.

J. C. Collins' arguments [see 72 n.] are used to support the contention that S used the original Latin version of *Menaechmi* and *Amphitruo* in *CE,* of *Mostellaria* and *Trinummus* in *TS,* and of *Miles gloriosus* in the characterization of Falstaff in *MW.*

(151)

Henneberger, O. P., *Proximate Sources for the Italianate Elements in Shakespeare,* Illinois, 1937, *passim.*

It is unnecessary to seek for sources of *CE* in *commedie dell' arte* [see 462]. *CE* was derived from *Menaechmi* and *Amphitruo.* Its title might have been suggested by Lambinus' annotated edition of *Menaechmi,* which notes as "*primus error,*" "*secundus error,*" *etc.,* each mistake in identity.

(152)

Labinski, Marianne, *Shakespeares Komödie der Irrungen: das Werk und seine Gestaltung auf der Bühne,* Breslau, 1934, pp. 16-38.

The influence of *Menaechmi* and *Amphitruo* upon *CE* is carefully analyzed. The following conclusion is drawn: there is insufficient evidence to support the hypothesis that S used either Warner's English translation of *Menaechmi* or some Italian version of that work.

(153)

Lea, K. M., *Italian Popular Comedy: A Study in the Commedia dell' Arte, 1560-1620, with Special Reference to the English Stage*, Oxford, 1934, II: 434-443.

CE might have been derived from *Menaechmi* in the Latin or in W. W.'s 1595 translation, or from a pre-Sn play based on Plautus. The last of these hypotheses is the most probable. Additional material for *CE* was derived from *Amphitruo*, IV, ii. Italianate features of *CE*, which might have been derived from *commedia dell' arte* sources, are noted. See 463.

(154)

McNiff, M. K., *The Menaechmi of Plautus and The Comedy of Errors*, MS Thesis, CL, 1917, 18 pp.

From an analysis of *Menaechmi* and *CE*, the conclusion is drawn that S improved upon the Plautine drama.

Menaechmi, The, see 157.

(155)

Robertson, J. M., *The Baconian Heresy*, pp. 197-198. See 18.

S did not read Plautus in the original. Either he obtained the plot of *CE* from a collaborator or from *The Historie of Error*.

(156)

Roeder, A. E. A. K., *Menechmi und Amphitruo im englischen Drama bis zur Restauration, 1661*, Leipzig, 1904, pp. 28-36.

That S was influenced by the plays of Plautus, either by seeing or reading them, is demonstrated by the echoes of *Mostellaria* and *Trinummus* in *TS*, of *Miles gloriosus* in *MW*, of *Rudens* in *Tem*, and of *Aulularia* in *MV*.

CE, too, was influenced, directly or indirectly, by *Menaechmi* and *Amphitruo*. To suggest a pre-Sn version of *CE* is futile. That S was influenced by Boisteau's tale of the two brothers of Avignon in *Histoires prodigeuses* is doubtful. Although some verbal parallels point to S's use of Warner's translation of *Menaechmi*, these are counterbalanced by the marked divergences between the characterizations in S's and in Warner's versions.

(157)

Rouse, W. H. D., ed., *The Menaechmi, the Original of Shakespeare's Comedy of Errors; the Latin Text Together with the Elizabethan Translation,* London, 1912, xiv, 122 pp.

A brief comparison of *Menaechmi* and *CE* is followed by a reprint of the original Latin and of the Warner translation.

(158)

Stronach, George, "Shakespeare's Scholarship." See 72.

As J. C. Collins has suggested, *CE* was influenced by *Mostellaria, Trinummus,* and *Miles gloriosus.* See 72 n.

(159)

Tannenbaum, S. A., "Notes on *The Comedy of Errors,*" *SJ*, 68 (1932): 103-124. [Sources, pp. 103-104.]

Three additional parallels are noted between *CE* and W. W.'s translation of *Menaechmi,* supplementing those listed in the 1907 Arden edition of *CE*.

(160)

Watt, H. A., "Plautus and Shakespeare: Further Comments on *Menaechmi* and *The Comedy of Errors,*" *Classical J*, 20 (1925): 401-407.

Willard Connely [see 142] errs in calling *CE* a poor imitation of *Menaechmi*. The social conditions and dramatic conventions under which they were written must be taken into consideration in a study of these two plays.

(161)

Wolff, M. J., "Shakespeare und die *Commedia dell' arte,*" *SJ*, 46 (1910): 1-20.

Divergences between *CE* and *Menaechmi* are listed to demonstrate that *CE* was written under Italianate influence.

See also 165 and 456.

INFLUENCE OF PLAUTUS ON SN PLAYS OTHER THAN *CE*

(162)

Forsythe, R. S., "A Plautine Source of *The Merry Wives of Windsor,*" *MP*, 18 (1920): 401-421.

Some material for *MW* was obtained from Tarlton's *Newes out of Purgatorie* and from Painter's *Palace of Pleasure*. For the plot and characters of

MW S was probably dependent upon Plautus' *Casina,* although there were few if any verbal borrowings from this source. The fact that S was acquainted with the Latin versions of *Menaechmi, Miles gloriosus, Amphitruo,* and *Mostellaria,* suggests that he read *Casina* in Latin. There may, however, have been a translation in manuscript, which is no longer extant. See also 511.

Plauti Mostellaria, see 164.

(163)

Smart, J. C., *Shakespeare: Truth and Tradition,* pp. 161-162. See 76.

Tranio and Grumio in *TS* were derived from *Mostellaria,* and characters in a number of Sn plays were dependent upon such Plautine types as the braggart, servant, and nurse.

(164)

Sonnenschein, E. A., ed., "Introduction" to *Plauti Mostellaria,* Oxford, 1907, pp. xvi-xvii.

Points of similarity between *TS* and *Mostellaria* are listed to show that S's dependence on this Plautine play is demonstrated not only by his use of the names of Grumio and Tranio, names which do not occur in *The Taming of a Shrew,* but also by the resemblances between the Tranios of the two plays.

(165)

Theobald, William, *The Classical Element in the Shakespeare Plays,* pp. 302-305. See 9.

The influence of *Menaechmi* and *Amphitruo* on over a half dozen Sn plays is noted.

See also 139, 144, 150, 156, 392, and 400.

Plinius, Caius Secundus (Pliny, The Elder)

FRENCH: [Books 7, 8] tr. Loys Meigret, Paris, 1543.
Le Second Livre, tr. Loys Meigret, Paris, 1552.
L'Histoire du monde, tr. A. du Pinet, Lyons, 1566.
Sommaire des singularitez de Pline by Pierre de Changy, Lyons, 1551.

ITALIAN: *Historia naturale,* tr. Cristoforo Landino, Venice, 1476.
Historia naturale, tr. Lodovico Domenichi, Venice, 1561.
Historia naturale, tr. Antonio Brucioli, Venice, 1548.

SPANISH: *Traduccion de los libros . . . de la historia natural* [tr. Hieronymus de Huerta], Madrid, 1599.

GERMAN: *Bücher und Schrifften von der Natur*, tr. J. Heyden, Frankfort on Main, 1565.

Natürlicher History, tr. H. von Eppendorf, Strassburg, 1543.

ENGLISH: *The Historie of the World*, tr. P. Holland, London, 1601.

A Summarie of the Antiquities and Wonders of the Worlde, out of the Sixtene First Bookes of Plinie, tr. I. A., London [1565].

See also **Solinus**. The geographical portion of his *Collectaneae rerum memorabilium* is an abstract of a treatise based on Pliny. See also Introduction, footnote 5.

(166)

Allen, D. C., "Hotspur's Earthquake," *MLN*, 50 (1935): 171-172.

The concept of the caged winds in *1H4*, III, i, 28-33, found ready acceptance in the middle ages and need not be credited to such classical sources as Pliny or Plutarch.

(167)

Baldwin, T. W., "A Note upon William Shakespeare's Use of Pliny" in *Essays in Dramatic Literature (the Parrott Presentation Volume)*, ed. Hardin Craig, Princeton, 1935, pp. 157-182.

Although S did not borrow from Pliny with sufficient frequency to suggest that he was a careful student of Pliny's writings, S's works show familiarity with certain passages tucked away in the original of Pliny which were ignored in the Holland translation. This seeming contradiction is to be explained by S's use of Dalecampius' index to Pliny, which led the dramatist directly to those Latin passages pertinent to his purpose. His task of translation was simplified by the use of Withal's Latin dictionary.

Parallels are cited *passim* to demonstrate that in some cases S depended upon Ovid's *Metamorphoses*, Vergil's *Aeneid*, or Erasmus' *Adagia* rather than, or in addition to, Pliny.

(168)

[Cowl, R. P.] *Sources of the Text of Henry the Fourth*, p. 43. See 15.

Among the possible sources of the description of Mars in *1H4*, IV, i, 116-117, were Pliny's *Natural History*, XXXVI, 4 and Lucan's *Pharsalia*, I, 444-445.

(169)

Draper, J. W., "The Realism of Shakespeare's Roman Plays," *SP*, 30 (1933): 225-242.

S's reference to the "thunder-stone" in *JC*, I, iii, 49, probably was not derived from Pliny's *Natural History*, XXXVI, lv.

(170)

French, J. M., "Othello among the Anthropophagi," *PMLA*, 49 (1934): 807-809.

S's use of "anthropophagi" was derived neither from Mandeville nor from Pliny but from the Renaissance maps accompanying Ptolemy's *Geography*. Other points in Othello's description (I, iii, 140-145) support this view. See 175.

(171)

Johnstone, J. E., "The Classical Element in Shakespeare." See 16.

S read Pliny in the original from which source he obtained his reference to henbane (*H*, I, v, 62).

(172)

Lathrop, H. B., "Shakespeare's Anthropophagi," *N*, 100 (1915): 76-77.

O, I, iii, 140-145 ("Wherin of anters . . .") was dependent upon Pierre de Changy's summary of Pliny, Lyons, 1551.

(173)

Owst, G. R., *Literature and Pulpit in Medieval England*, Cambridge, 1933, pp. 591-592, 536 n.

Francis Douce erred in crediting *KL*, IV, vi, 183 ff. ("we came crying hither . . .") to Pliny. It was derived from the Bible: "Book of Wisdom," VII, 3.

(174)

Sandys, J. E., "Scholarship" in *Shakespeare's England*, p. 265. See 12.

From Holland's translation of Pliny, II, 97, S derived the allusion to the Pontic Sea in *O*, III, iii, 454-457. The description of a new born infant in *KL*, IV, vi, 183 ff., was suggested by Holland's Proeme, VII.

(175)

Stroup, T. B., "Shakespeare's Use of a Travel-Book Commonplace," *PQ*, 17 (1938): 351-358.

Othello's description of cannibals and headless men (*O*, I, iii, 140-145) need be attributed neither to the influence of Mandeville nor to Pliny nor to the maps of Ptolemy. These concepts were commonplaces in the Elizabethan period. See 170.

(176)

Theobald, William, *The Classical Element in the Shakespeare Plays*, pp. 305-316. See 9.

About a score of Sn passages are listed that were dependent on Pliny, whose work S read in translation.

See also 464.

Saxo Grammaticus

Saxo Grammaticus' *History of the Danes* is usually considered as an ultimate source of *H*. There are only one or two cursory references to it as a possible direct source.

See 361.

Seneca, Lucius Annaeus

Prose

FRENCH: *Euvres* [epistles, *etc.*] tr. Laurens Premierfaict, Paris [1500].
Les Œuvres, tr. Antoine Du Verdier [no pl.], 1584.
Œuvres [tr. Simon Goulart], Paris, 1598.
Œuvres, tr. Mathieu de Chalvet, Paris, 1604.
Les Authoritez, sentences et singuliers enseignements [Latin and French], tr. P. Grognet, Paris, 1534.
De la clemence, tr. A. Cappel, Paris, 1578.
Epistres, tr. Le seigneur de Pressac, Paris, 1582.
Autres vingt epistres [no tr.], Tours, 1594.

SPANISH: *Cinco libros* [tr. Alonso de Cartagena], Seville, 1491.
Los cinco libros, tr. Pedro Diaz de Toledo [no pl.], 1530.
Cinco libros [no tr.], Antwerp, 1551.
Siete libros, tr. Pt. Fernandez Navarrete, Madrid, 1601.
Flores de Seneca, tr. Juan Martin Cordero, Antwerp, 1555.
Las epistolas, tr. Fernan Perez de Guzman, Saragossa, 1496.
Las epistolas [tr. L. Arietino], Toledo, 1510.

ITALIAN: *Pistole*, tr. Sebastiano Manilio, Venice, 1494.

GERMAN: *Zuchtbücher*, tr. Michael Herr, Strassburg, 1540. [Contains some epistles and several tracts, including *De clementia*.]

ENGLISH: *The Woorke of . . . Seneca, Concerning Benefyting,* tr. A. Golding, London, 1578.

De remediis fortuitorum, Latin and English, tr. R. Whyttynton, London, 1547.

Tragedies

ENGLISH: *The Sixt Tragedie . . . Entituled Troas,* tr. Jasper Heywood, London, 1559.

The Seconde Tragedie . . . Thyestes, tr. J. Heywood, London, 1560.

Tragedia prima, Hercules furens, Latin and English, tr. Jasper Heywood, London, 1561.

The Lamentable Tragedie of Œdipus, tr. A. Nevyle, London, 1563.

The Seventh Tragedie . . . Medea, tr. I. Studley, London, 1566.

The Eyght Tragedie . . . Agamemnon, tr. I. Studley, London, 1566.

The Ninth Tragedie . . . Called Octavia, tr. T. N[uce], London [1566].

Seneca, His Tenne Tragedies [tr. J. Heywood and others], London, 1581.

INFLUENCE OF SENECAN TRAGEDY ON S

(177)

Alexander, Peter, *Shakespeare's Henry VI and Richard III,* p. 140. See 139.

Most of the melodramatic situations in *Titus* were derived from Seneca's tragedies.

(178)

Boyer, C. V., *The Villain as Hero in Elizabethan Tragedy,* London, 1914, *passim.*

The parallel between *R3,* IV, ii, 63 ff. ("Uncertain way of gain! But I am in So far in blood . . .") and *Agamemnon,* 116, is striking. However, the strong similarity between the mood in Senecan tragedy and in *R3* may be merely coincidental. J. W. Cunliffe's arguments notwithstanding, there is little resemblance between the hero-villains of Seneca and Shakespeare. [Note: Since J. W. Cunliffe's analysis of the problem precedes 1904, it does not fall within the scope of this bibliography.]

(179)

Bradley, A. C., *Shakespearean Tragedy,* London, New York, 1904, pp. 389-390.

Parallels are cited to show the influence of Seneca on *Mac, AYL,* and *MND.* See 129.

(180)

Creizenach, Wilhelm, *The English Drama in the Age of Shakespeare*, p. 74. See 106.

Mac, II, ii, 61 ff. ("Will all great Neptune's ocean . . .") is a clear reminiscence of Seneca.

(181)

Dowlin, C. M., "Two Shakspere Parallels in Studley's Translation of Seneca's *Agamemnon*," *SAB*, 14 (1939) : 256.

W. R.'s prefatory verses to Studley's translation of *Agamemnon* contain the line: "One hurlye burlye done, another doth begin." This served as the source of the line in *Mac*, I, i, 3 ("When the hurlyburly's done . . ."). Another Sn parallel to Seneca is noted, but it is discarded as a source possibility.

(182)

Eliot, T. S., "Introduction" to *Seneca His Tenne Tragedies*, ed. Thomas Newton, London, 1927, I: v-liv. [Reprinted as T. S. Eliot, "Seneca in Elizabethan Translation," *Selected Essays*, New York, 1932, pp. 51-88.]

Among Sn plays which were deeply influenced by Senecan language and apparatus, though not by Senecan form, are *R2* and *R3*. The horrors in *Titus* were the result of the influence of contemporary Italy rather than of Seneca.

(183)

Eliot, T. S., *Shakespeare and the Stoicism of Seneca, an Address Read before the Shakespeare Association, March 18, 1927*, London, 1927, 17 pp. [Reprinted in T. S. Eliot, *Selected Essays*, New York, 1932, pp. 107-120.]

Some Senecan influence can be seen in S's writings, although some of it might have been indirect. There is little likelihood that S was acquainted with Seneca's prose, and none that he accepted the Senecan outlook on life.

(184)

Fansler, H. E.,*The Evolution of Technic in Elizabethan Tragedy*, Chicago, 1914, *passim*.

Scattered references allude to the Senecan influence in *R3*, *RJ*, and *JC*.

(185)

Godley, A. D., "Senecan Tragedy" in *English Literature and the Classics*, lectures collected by G. S. Gordon, pp. 228-246. See 124.

S and Seneca had many ideas in common, but these were popularly held concepts which were current in S's period. There is no justification, for example, for suggesting that *Mac*, V, iii, 22 ff. ("I have liv'd long enough . . .") was derived from *Hercules furens*, 1258-1262.

(186)

Koeppel, E., "Bottoms 'Ercles' und Studleys Übersetzung von Senecas *Hercules Œtaeus*," *SJ*, 47 (1911) : 190-191.

Bottom's use of alliteration and his references to Hercules in *MND*, I, ii and *MND*, V, i, were intended to ridicule Studley's translations of Seneca's *Hercules furens* and *Hercules Œtaeus*.

(187)

Koeppel, E., "Randglossen zu dem Andersschen Werk über Shakespeares Belesenheit," p. 49. See 120.

Lady Macbeth's monologue upon receiving word of the king's impending visit to Inverness (*Mac*, I, v) was derived, not from Seneca as H. R. D. Anders suggests, but from *The Misfortunes of Arthur*.

(188)

Koeppel, E., "Shakespeares *Richard III* und Senecas *Troades*," *SJ*, 47 (1911) : 188-190.

The scene of the three mourning queens in *R3*, IV, iv, was not based on medieval drama, but on the scene of Helena, Andromache, and Hecuba in Seneca's *Troades*.

(189)

Kröger, Ernst, *Die Sage von Macbeth bis zu Shakspere*, p. 228 and *passim*. See 39.

The ghost of Banquo and *Mac*, I, v, 41 ff. ("Come, you spirits . . .") were derived from Seneca's *Medea*. See also 121.

(190)

Lucas, F. L., *Seneca and Elizabethan Tragedy*, Cambridge, 1922, pp. 117-123.

Senecan influence on S has been grossly exaggerated. Although S read Seneca's works, perhaps even in the original, most of the resemblances to Seneca that have been noted in *Titus*, *R3*, *Mac*, *H*, *2H4*, *2H6*, and *3H6* are examples of mere coincidence rather than of actual borrowing.

(191)

Ploch, Georg, "Über den Dialog in den Dramen Shakespeares und seiner Vorläufer" in *Giessener Beiträge zur Erforschung der Sprache und Kultur Englands und Nord-Amerikas,* ed. Wilhelm von Horn, Vol. II, Giessen, 1925, pp. 129-192. [Especially pp. 184-190.]

In a discussion of the development of dramatic dialogue in sixteenth-century England, there are scattered references to the influence of Senecan literary devices, such as stichomythia, on the early plays of S.

(192)

Sandys, J. E., "Education" and "Scholarship" in *Shakespeare's England,* pp. 235, 260-261. See 12 and 41.

There is no absolute proof that S read Seneca even though Seneca's *Phaedra* is directly quoted in *Titus* (IV, i, 81-82 and II, i, 133 ff.), since S's authorship of this play is frequently questioned. Suggestions of Senecan influence on *Mac, KJ,* and *H* are also noted, but no definite conclusion is drawn regarding them.

(193)

Schaubert, Else v., "Die Stelle vom 'rauhen Pyrrhus'. . . ." See 129.

Although S read Seneca, at least in English translation, the Senecan influence in *H* came *via* the pre-Sn *Hamlet,* and in *KL via* Sidney. Although Bradley may be correct in his suggestion of Seneca's *Hippolytus* as the source of some passages in *AYL* and *MND,* S could have obtained this material from English sources. *Mac,* II, ii, 61 ff. ("Will all great Neptune's ocean . . .") was not necessarily derived from Seneca.

(194)

Schmidt, Karl, *Margaret von Anjou vor und bei Shakespeare (Palaestra 54),* Berlin, 1906, pp. 252, 286.

Although Margaret's relationship to Henry VI was described in the chronicles, S's conception of Margaret was also stimulated by reminiscences of Seneca's *Medea.*

Seneca His Tenne Tragedies, see 182.

(195)

Spearing, E. M., *The Elizabethan Translations of Seneca's Tragedies,* Cambridge, 1912, p. 12 and n. [Reprinted in extended form from *MLR,* 4 (1909) : 437-461.]

Even as late as in the period of his tragedies, S was influenced by the Senecan tragedies in English translation. The ghost of Hamlet's father is very similar to the ghost of Thyestes in Seneca's *Agamemnon*.

(196)

Spearing, E. M., "Introduction" to *Studley's Translations of Seneca's Agamemnon and Medea, Edited from the Octavos of 1566*, ed. E. M. Spearing, Louvain, 1913, pp. vii-xxiii. [*H*, pp. xvii-xxii.]

Studley's translation of Seneca probably influenced *H*, directly or indirectly. This influence might have been derived from the strongly Senecan *Ur-Hamlet* of Kyd, which was toned down by S. The parallels between *Hamlet* and *Agamemnon* are cited in detail.

(197)

Theobald, William, *The Classical Element in the Shakespeare Plays*, pp. 323-327. See 9.

Parallels between a number of Sn and Senecan plays are cited.

(198)

Wilhelm, Friedrich, "Zu Seneca und Shakespeare *(Richard III)*," *Ar*, 129 (1912): 69-73.

Detailed parallels are cited between *R3* and several Senecan plays. However, it is uncertain whether S depended in these instances directly upon Seneca or upon Legge's *Ricardus Tertius*.

See also 491.

INFLUENCE OF SENECAN PROSE ON S

(199)

Review: Brandl, A., "John M. Robertson, *Montaigne and Shakespeare*," *SJ*, 46 (1910): 272-273.

Portia's speech on mercy (*MV*, IV, i, 184 ff.) was not necessarily derived from Seneca, despite E. A. Sonnenschein's arguments to that effect. [See 206, 207, 208, and 209.] It might have been derived from the homily on mercifulness in Elyot's *Governour*, II, vii, or from Peele or Spenser. See 28 n.

(200)

Eidson, J. O., "A Senecan Parallel in *Hamlet*," *SAB*, 10 (1935): 105.

There is a parallel between *H*, II, ii, 259 ff. ("Why, then, 'tis none to you . . .") and Seneca's *Quaestiones naturales*, III, preface, and *Epistles*, IX, 21-22 and LXXVIII, 13.

(201)

Enk, P. J., "Shakespeare's 'Small Latin.'" See 144.

E. A. Sonnenschein is correct in suggesting Seneca as the source of Portia's speech on mercy. See 206, 207, 208, and 209.

(202)

Greenwood, G. G., *Is There a Shakespeare Problem?* p. 151. See 64.

E. A. Sonnenschein is correct in suggesting Seneca as the source of Portia's speech on mercy. See 206, 207, 208, and 209.

(203)

Greenwood, G. G., *The Shakespeare Problem Restated*, pp. 94-96. See 65.

The same observation is made as in 202.

(204)

Hewlett, J. H., *The Influence of Seneca's Epistulae Morales on Elizabethan Tragedy*, MS Thesis, U of Chicago, 1931, *passim*.

A number of parallels are cited to demonstrate the influence of Seneca's letters on S's works.

(205)

Keller, Wolfgang and Cläre Hunekuhl, "Antike Anleihen bei Shakespeare," *SJ*, 59-60 (1924): 221-222.

Despite P. J. Enk, Seneca was not, necessarily, the source of Portia's speech on mercy. P. J. Enk is, however, justified in crediting S with a knowledge of Plautus' *Amphitruo, Menaechmi,* and *Mostellaria*. There is no proof of S's having been dependent on Plautus' *Captivi,* the parallels being idealogical rather than verbal. See 144 and 201.

(206)

Sonnenschein, E. A., "Latin as an Intellectual Force in Civilisation," *National R,* 47 (1906): 670-683. [Seneca and S, pp. 682-683.]

Seneca's *De clementia* was the source of Portia's speech on mercy (*MV*, IV, i, 184 ff.) and of *H*, II, ii, 561 ff. ("use every man . . ."). Since no English translation of this work had been written before *MV* was composed, S must have read the Senecan essay in Latin. See 199, 201, 202, 203, and 211.

(207)

Sonnenschein, E. A., "Shakespeare's Knowledge of Latin," *TLS*, March 17, 1921, pp. 179-180.

S probably read Seneca's *De clementia,* source of Portia's speech on mercy, in the original Latin, although he could also have obtained it in French and in German translation. See 199, 201, 202, 203, and 211.

(208)

Sonnenschein, E. A., "Shakespeare's Knowledge of Latin," *TLS*, April 28, 1921, p. 276.

Although Elyot's *Governour,* II, vii; Spenser's *Amoretti,* xlix; and *Edward the Third,* V, i, 42-43, contain elements of Portia's speech on mercy, all of these elements were united only in Seneca. Montaigne echoed many of these Senecan sentiments, but a point omitted in Montaigne—regarding the absence of war—occurred both in Seneca and in S. *Tem* was influenced by both Seneca and Montaigne, but there is no evidence that it was dependent on the Lodge translation of Seneca. See 199, 201, 202, 203, and 211.

(209)

Sonnenschein, E. A., "Shakspere and Stoicism." See 29.

Seneca's *De clementia,* in the original Latin, influenced Portia's speech on mercy in *MV,* IV, i, 184 ff.; *MM,* II, ii, 59 ff. ("No ceremony that to great ones 'longs . . ."); *H,* II, ii, 561 ff. ("use every man . . ."); *KL,* IV, vi, 165 ff. ("Thou rascal beadle . . ."); and, perhaps, *Titus,* I, i, 117 ff. ("Wilt thou draw near the nature of the gods? . . ."). See 199, 201, 202, 203, and 211.

(210)

Stopes, C. C. [Correspondence], *New Sna,* 6 (1907) : 73.

The suggestion that S obtained some suggestions for *H* from Seneca's *De clementia* is unjustified. The same ideas are treated in Sir John Conway's *Meditations and Prayers.*

(211)

Stopes, C. C., "Shakespeare's Knowledge of Latin," *TLS,* March 24, 1921, p. 196.

Although S might have resorted to some translation of Seneca which is no longer extant, E. A. Sonnenschein's general hypothesis is correct. [See 206,

207, 208, and 209.] However, a passage resembling Portia's mercy speech may also be found in Sir John Conway's *Meditations and Prayers* and in his *Posy of Flowered Praiers.*

(212)

Vollhardt, W., "Italienische Parallelen zu Shakespeares *Hamlet,*" *SJ,* 62 (1926) : 132-157.

Alois Brandl has overemphasized the influence of Seneca on *H.* Seneca's writings, however, especially his epistles, might have suggested the "To be, or not to be" soliloquy and some other *H* passages.

See also 93 and 94.

Seneca The Elder

(213)

Wilder, M. L., "Shakespeare's 'Small Latin,' " *MLN,* 40 (1925) : 380-381.

Two passages in *1H4* resemble Seneca's *Controversiae* so closely as to suggest S's having borrowed from this source. The parallels exist between *1H4,* II, iii, 115-116 ("for I well believe Thou wilt not utter what thou dost not know") and *Controversiae,* II, v, 12; and between *1H4,* II, iii, 42 ff. (Lady Percy's description of Hotspur's secretiveness) and *Controversiae,* II, v, 20. See 345.

"Sententiae Pueriles," see under Culmann

Solinus, Caius Julius

ENGLISH: *The Excellent and Pleasant Worke of Julius Solinus,* tr. Arthur Golding, Gent., London, 1587.

See also **Pliny.**

(214)

Gray, Arthur, *"The Comedy of Errors."* See 114.

S probably derived the name Solinus in *CE* from the title of Golding's translation of Solinus. There is no evidence whatever that S was acquainted with the Latin of Solinus, and little evidence that he was acquainted with the text of the translation.

Spagnuoli, see Baptista Mantuanus

Suetonius, Tranquilius Caius

FRENCH: *Lucan, Suétone, et Saluste* [no tr.], Paris, 1490.
Suetone translaté en françois by Gu. Michel dit de Tours, Paris, 1520.
La Vie des douze Caesars, tr. George de la Boutiere, Lyons, 1556.

ITALIAN: *Le vite de' dodici Cesari*, tr. Paolo del Rosso, Rome, 1544.
Le vite dei dieci imperatori, tr. Mambrino Roseo, Venice, 1544.

SPANISH: *Las vidas de los doze Cesares*, tr. Iaimus Bartholomaeus, Tarragona, 1596.

ENGLISH: *History of the 12 Caesars*, tr. Philemon Holland, London, 1606.

(215)

Theobald, William, *The Classical Element in the Shakespeare Plays*, p. 348. See 9.

Passages in Suetonius are cited as the source of lines in *JC* and *H*.

See also 26 and 30.

Tacitus, Caius Cornelius

FRENCH: *Les Œuvres* [tr. C. Fauchet and E. de la Planche], Paris, 1582.
Œuvres, tr. P. D. B., Paris, 1599.
Selections in *Harangues militaires*, tr. F. de Belleforest, Paris, 1573.
[Selections in *Preface sur la mort de son beaupère . . . les calamités advenues aux hommes de lettres . . . quelques harangues*] tr. François Douynet, Troyes, 1580.

ITALIAN: *Gli annali* [with history], tr. Giorgio Dati, Venice, 1563.
Annali ed istorie, tr. Adriano Politi, Venice, 1604.
Il primo libro degli annali, tr. B. Davanzati, Florence, 1596.
L'Imperio di Tiberio Cesare, tr. B. Davanzati, Florence, 1600.

GERMAN: *Der römischen Keyser Historien* [Annals and Histories] tr. J. Micyllus, Mainz, 1535.
Selections in *Ain Büchlin das durch die natürlichen Mayster Aristotelem, Avicennam, Galienum, Albertum und andern natürlichen Maystern von mancherlay seltzamen wunderlichen fragenbeschriben . . .* [no tr.] Freiburg, 1500.

ENGLISH: *The Ende of Nero and Beginning of Galba: Fower Bookes of the Histories of Cornelius Tacitus, the Life of Agricola* [tr. H. Savile], London, 1591.

The Annales . . . the Description of Germanie, tr. R. Grenewey, London, 1598.

The Ende of Nero, etc. The Life of Agricola, tr. H. Smith, London, 1605.

Annales, XII, 51, tr. William Painter, *The Palace of Pleasure,* II, xiv, London, 1566.

(216)

[Cowl, R. P.] *Sources of the Text of Henry the Fourth,* p. 41. See 15.

Tacitus, *Annales,* XIV, xi, in the Grenewey translation, influenced *1H4,* I, iii, 30 ff. ("when the fight was done . . .").

(217)

Johnstone, J. E., "The Classical Influence in Shakespeare." See 16.

The influence of Tacitus on S's sonnets is noted in passing.

(218)

Theobald, William, *The Classical Element in the Shakespeare Plays,* pp. 350-354. See 9.

Parallels are noted between Tacitus and passages in *R2, R3, H5, 3H6,* and *AC.*

See also 30.

Terentius, Afer Publius

FRENCH: *Le Grant Therence en francoys* [tr. Guillaume Rippe?], Paris, 1539.

Comédies [tr. Jean Bourlier], Antwerp, 1566.
Comédies, tr. M. Ant. de Muret, Paris, 1583.

ITALIAN: *Le comedie di Terentio volgari,* tr. J-B. da Borgo-Franco, Venice, 1546.
Comedia detta gli Adelfi, tr. Alb. Lollio, Venice, 1554.
Li fratelli, tr. Fr. Corte, Mantua, 1554.

SPANISH: *Las seys comedias,* tr. Petrus Simon Abril, Saragossa, 1577.

GERMAN: *Sechs verteutschte Comedien,* tr. Valent Bolz, Tubingen, 1540.

Sechs Comödien, tr. J. Episcopius (Bischoff), Frankfort on Main, 1568.
Terentii deutsche Schauspiele, tr. Michel Bapst, Leipzig, 1596.

ENGLISH: *Terence in English fabulae Anglicae factae opera* [Latin and English], tr. R. B[ernard], London, 1598.
Andria, tr. M. Kyffin, London, 1588.

Nicolas Udall, *Floures for Latine Spekynge Selected and Gathered out of Terence,* London, 1533.

See also Introduction, footnote 5.

(219)

Creizenach, Wilhelm, *The English Drama in the Age of Shakespeare,* p. 74. See 106.

Adelphi, 832 ff. is parallel to *H,* II, i, 114 ff. ("By heaven, it is as proper to our age . . .").

(220)

Gray, Arthur, *"The Comedy of Errors."* See 114.

S derived the names Antipholus and Dromio from Terentian comedy.

(221)

Robertson, J. M., *The Baconian Heresy,* p. 212. See 18.

MV, II, ii, 42 ff. ("Turn up on your right hand . . .") was not derived from *Adelphi,* IV, ii. It is merely an example of spontaneous fooling.

(222)

Theobald, William, *The Classical Element in the Shakespeare Plays,* pp. 354-357. See 9.

Heautontimorumenos, Andria, Adelphi, and *Eunuchus* influenced passages in over a half dozen Sn plays.

(223)

Tschernjajew, Paul, "Shakespeare und Terenz," *A,* 55 (1931): 282-295.

Borrowings from Terence in over twenty Sn plays are cited to demonstrate S's great indebtedness to the Latin dramatist.

See also 456, 462, and 550.

Tully, see **Cicero**

Velleius Paterculus, Caius

(224)

Theobald, William, *The Classical Element in the Shakespeare Plays,* pp. 369-370. See 9.

Passages in *TC, H,* and *Mac* are cited to demonstrate the influence of Velleius on S.

See also 30.

Vergilius Maro, Publius

ENGLISH: "Here fynnyssheth the boke yf Eneydos" [an abstract rather than a tr. by William Caxton, Westminster, 1490].

The XIII Bukes of Eneados, tr. into Scottish meter by G. Douglas, London, 1553.

Certain Bokes [2, 4] *of Virgiles Aeneis,* tr. Henry Earle of Surrey, London, 1557.

The First Foure Bookes of Virgil's Aeneis, tr. R. Stanyhurst, London, 1583.

The Thirteene Bookes of Aeneidos, tr. T. Phaer and T. Twyne, London, 1583.

The Bukoliks . . . Together with . . . Georgics, tr. A. F[raunce or Fleming], London, 1589.

"The Lamentation of Corydon for the Loss of Alexis," tr. A. Fraunce in *The Countesse of Pembrokes Yvychurch,* London, 1591.

"Culex," tr. Edmund Spenser in *Complaints, Containing Sundrie Small Poemes of the Worlds Vanitie,* London, 1596.

See also Introduction, footnote 5.

(225)

Berdan, J. M., "Shakespeare's Learning," *N,* 92 (1911): 241.

Baconians have made various erudite suggestions regarding the source of the "Hyrcan" tigers in *Mac,* III, iv, 101; *3H6,* I, iv, 155; and *H,* II, ii, 481. Actually, the word echoes *The Aeneid,* IV, 367 (*"Caucasus, Hyrcaneaque admorunt ubera tigres"*). Since the word "Hyrcan" appears in neither Surrey's nor Stanyhurst's translation, S must have derived the word from the original Latin version. Acquaintance with the fourth book of *The Aeneid* during the Renaissance cannot, however, be considered proof of extraordinary erudition.

(226)

Bond, R. W., "The Framework of *The Comedy of Errors*," *Studia Otiosa*,
London, 1938, p. 44 n.

Phaer's translation of Vergil might have suggested to S the following
passages in *Tem:* I, ii, 418 ("Most sure, the goddess") ; the references to
the widow Dido and to the Harpy, II, i, *passim* and III, iii, 83; and the
masque of Juno, Iris, and Ceres, IV, i.

(227)

Carruthers, C. H., "The Shakespearian Ducdame," *PQ,* 12 (1933) : 37-43.

The phrase containing the word "ducdame" (*AYL,* II, v, 54, 58) is a
vulgarization of Vergil's eighth eclogue of the *Bucolics.* This eclogue had
become popular as a magic incantation.

(228)

Colvin, Sidney, "The Sack of Troy in Shakespeare's *Lucrece* and in Some
Fifteenth Century Drawings and Tapestries" in *A Book of Homage
to Shakespeare,* pp. 88-99. See 57.

S or the painter, whose work S described in *Lucrece,* derived the story of
Sinon and the description of Troy directly from Vergil.

(229)

Conway, R. S., "The Classical Elements in Shakespeare's *Tempest*," *New
Studies of a Great Inheritance,* London, 1921, pp. 165-189.

Many passages in *Tem* were influenced by *The Aeneid,* especially by Book
I, and by *Georgics* I. Reminiscences of the latter, combined with suggestions
obtained from Montaigne, served as the basis of the Gonzalo speech on an
ideal commonwealth.

(230)

[Cowl, R. P.] *Sources of the Text of Henry the Fourth, passim.* See 15.

Lines in Vergil are suggested as the source of passages in *1* and *2H4.*

(231)

Greenwood, G. G., *Is There a Shakespeare Problem?* pp. 130-134, 145.
See 64.

Vergil influenced several passages in *Tem.*

(232)

Greenwood, G. G., *The Shakespeare Problem Restated,* pp. 94, 96-97. See 65.

J. C. Collins [see 72 n.] makes too weak a case for the Vergilian influence in S. Several passages in *Tem* are cited which show the influence of Vergil.

(233)

Haynes, French, "Shakespeare and the Troy Story." See 117.
The influence of Vergil on S is analyzed, with special stress on the borrowings in *TC.*

(234)

Jaggard, William, *Shakespeare Once a Printer and Bookman,* p. 27. See 2.
S alludes to *The Aeneid* several times, as in *H,* II, ii, 476 and in *AC,* IV, xii, 53.

(235)

Johnstone, J. E., "The Classical Element in Shakespeare." See 16.

A line of Vergil not yet in translation, *"Flectere si nequeo superos, Acheronta movebo,"* was translated by S in *Titus* (IV, iii, 50) as "We will solicit heaven and move the gods."

(236)

Robertson, J. M., *The Baconian Heresy,* pp. 192-194, 210. See 18.

Even if S had studied Vergil at school, he was not necessarily a classicist. Neither *Tem,* I, ii, 418 ("Most sure, the goddess") nor *CE,* I, i, 31-32 ("A heavier task . . .") was derived from Vergil.

(237)

Sandys, J. E., "Education" in *Shakespeare's England,* p. 235. See 41.
Vergil's *"Tantaene animis . . . ,"* (*Aeneid,* I, 11) was accurately quoted in *2H6,* II, i, 24. *2H6,* IV, i, 117 blended *Aeneid,* VII, 446 with Ovid's *Metamorphoses,* III, 40.

(238)

Theobald, William, *The Classical Element in the Shakespeare Plays,* pp. 370-386. See 9.

A generous list of parallel passages is offered to demonstrate S's dependence upon *The Aeneid, Georgics, Eclogues,* and *Culex.*

See also 100, 110, 130, and 167.

Vives, Luis

(239)

Watson, Foster, "Shakespeare and Two Stories of Luis Vives," *19* C, 85 (1919) : 297-306.

From Vives' *Fabula de homine,* S might have derived *AYL,* II, vii, 137 ff. ("This wide and universal theatre . . .") and *H,* II, ii, 323 ff. ("What a piece of work is a man . . ."). S probably obtained the theme of the *TS* Induction either from a letter which Vives wrote to Francis, Duke of Béjar, or from Richard Edwards' collection, *The Waking Man's Dream,* 1570.

CHAPTER TWO

Influence of Greek Literature on Shakespeare

Achilles Tatius

ENGLISH: *The Most Delectable History of Clitophon and Leucippe,* tr W. B[urton], London, 1597.

(240)

Perott, Joseph de, "Eine portugiesische Parallele zum *Heiligen Dreikönigs-abend," A,* 38 (1914) : 255-260.

The swift reconciliation in *TGV,* which has been frequently censured by critics, might have been suggested by the quick forgiveness accorded to the wicked Kallisthenes in *Clitophon and Leucippe.* In *TN* the disguise motif was combined with some of the elements found in this Greek romance which gave S the inspiration for Malvolio. Some of the comic scenes of *TN,* however, are suggestive of Giovan Maria Cecchi's *L'Ossiuolo.*

(241)

Perott, Joseph de, "Noch eine eventuelle Quelle zum *Heiligen Dreikönigs-abend," SJ,* 46 (1910) : 118-120.

Similarities are noted between *Clitophon and Leucippe* and *TN.* Certain details of *TN,* not to be found in this romance, are in the Italian comedy: *I morti vivi* of Sforza d'Oddi.

See also 570.

Aelianus, Claudius

ENGLISH: *A Registre of Hystories,* tr. A. Fleming, London, 1576. William Painter, *The Palace of Pleasure,* London, 1566, I, viii-x.

(242)

Jaggard, William, *Shakespeare Once a Printer and Bookman,* pp. 26-27. See 2.

From Fleming's translation of Aelian, S could have learned the legend of Tereus alluded to in *Cym*, II, ii, 44 ff. ("She hath been reading late The tale of Tereus . . .") and in *Titus*, IV, i, 47 ff. ("This is the tragic tale of Philomel, And treats of Tereus' treason . . .").

(243)

Koeppel, E., "Randglossen zu dem Andersschen Werk über Shakespeares Belesenheit," p. 49. See 120.

H. R. D. Anders should have included Fleming's translation of Aelian among the books S read. It is mentioned in F. J. Furnivall's "The End of Hamlet's Sea of Troubles," *Academy*, 35 (1889) : 360.

(244)

Robertson, J. M., *The Baconian Heresy*, p. 244. See 18.

RJ, IV, iv, 11 ff. ("Ay, you have been a mouse-hunt . . .") was not derived from Aelian, despite William Theobald to the contrary. See 245.

(245)

Theobald, William, *The Classical Element in the Shakespeare Plays*, pp. 59-61. See 9.

Passages from *AC*, *H*, *RJ*, *Tem*, and *TC* are cited which suggest S's dependence upon Aelian. See 244.

Aeschylus

LATIN: *Tragoediae sex*, tr. Johannes Sanravius, Basel, 1555.
Tragoediae selectae Aeschyli, Sophoclis, Euripidis [tr. Erasmus, Buchanan, *et al.*, no pl.], 1567.
Septem Thebana tragoedia, tr. Q. S. F. Christianus, Paris, 1585.

(246)

Robertson, J. M., *The Baconian Heresy*, pp. 247-248. See 18.

H, III, i, 59 ("sea of troubles") was not derived from Aeschylus but was an Elizabethan commonplace.

(247)

Theobald, William, *The Classical Element in the Shakespeare Plays*, pp. 61-66. See 9.

A score of Sn passages are cited which might have been dependent upon Aeschylus' plays.

See also 264, 310, and 353.

Aesop

ENGLISH: *The Book of the Subtyl Historyes and Fables of Esope*, tr. W. Caxton, Westminster, 1484.

The Morall Fabillis of Esope in Scottis Meter be Maister Henrisone, Edinburgh, 1570.

Aesopz Fablz in Tru Ortography, tr. W. Bullokar, London, 1585.

See also Introduction, footnote 5.

(248)

Anders, Heinrich, "Randglossen zu *Shakespeare's Belesenheit,*" *SJ*, 62 (1926) : 158-162.

In writing *TC*, III, iii, 145 ("Time hath, my lord, a wallet at his back"), S had in mind Aesop's fable of the two wallets which Jupiter gave to man.

(249)

Crundell, H. W., "Shakespeare, Lyly, and Aesop," *NQ*, 168 (1935): 312.

The Aesopian version of the Scarabeus tale is found in *Cym*, III, iii, 19 ff. ("And often, to our comfort . . ."). *2H6*, IV, i, 101 ff. ("reproach and beggary Is crept . . .") was intended as a satire on the Lylian version of this tale in *Endimion*, V, i, 129 ff. ("There might I beholde Drones or Beetles . . .").

(250)

Theobald, William, *The Classical Element in the Shakespeare Plays*, p. 66. See 9.

MM, I, iii, 22 ("Even like an o'ergrown lion . . .") was suggested to S by Aesop's fable of the old lion who, too weak to pursue his prey, ate the animals who came to visit him.

Alessandrino, see Achilles Tatius

Antoninus, Aurelius, see **Aurelius Antoninus**

Appian

ENGLISH: *An Auncient Historie and Exquisite Chronicle of the Romanes Warres,* two parts [second part tr. W. B.], London, 1578.

(251)

Review: "Boecker, Alexander, *A Probable Italian Source of Shakespeare's Julius Caesar,*" *Ar,* 132 (1914) : 243.

Alexander Boecker's thesis that Pescetti was a source of *JC* is weak. His exposition has, however, made clearer the possibility of Appian as a source of S's play. See 501.

(252)

Lathrop, H. B., *Translations from the Classics,* pp. 180-182. See 69.

From W. B.'s translation of Appian, S gleaned several passages which he used in *JC.*

(253)

MacCallum, M. W., *Shakespeare's Roman Plays and Their Background,* London, 1910, pp. 644-652.

The 1578 English translation of Appian probably influenced such passages in *AC* as III, v, 17 ff. ("He's walking in the garden . . ."). Despite certain discrepancies between Appian's and S's accounts, Appian might have supplemented Plutarch as a source for Antony's speech in *JC,* III, ii, 79 ff. ("Friends, Romans, countrymen . . .").

(254)

Theobald, William, *The Classical Element in the Shakespeare Plays,* pp. 74-75. See 9.

AC, IV, iii, 15 (" 'Tis the God Hercules . . .") and *JC,* II, ii, 109 ("Welcome, Publius") were influenced by Appian.

See also 30 and 501.

Aristophanes

LATIN AND GREEK-AND-LATIN: *Nicodemi Frischlini Aristophanes,* Frankfort on Main, 1586. [Contains *Plutus, The Knights, The Clouds, The Frogs, The Acharnians.*]

Comoediae undecim, tr. Andreas Divus, Basel, 1539.

Q. S. F. Christiani in A. Irenam vel pacem, Paris, 1589.

Plutus [tr. F. Passius], Parma, 1501; Also tr. T. Venatorius, Nuremberg, 1531; M. Cabedius, Paris, 1547; C. Girardus, Paris, 1549.

ITALIAN: *Comedie,* tr. Bm. and Pt. Rositini, Venice, 1545.

(255)

Chapman, Arthur, "Shakespeare and Aristophanes," *The Academy,* 72 (1907): 123.

H, III, ii, 400 ff. ("Do you see yonder cloud . . .") was not dependent upon *The Clouds* of Aristophanes. Not only is the thought which they have in common a usual one, but their application of that thought is markedly different. See 256.

(256)

Hill, N. W., "Shakespeare and Aristophanes," *The Academy,* 72 (1907): 76.

Aristophanes' *The Clouds,* 345-348, was the source of *H,* III, ii, 400 ff. The resemblance is more marked in the second quarto than in the first. Perhaps the discrepancy between the two quartos is to be explained by the fact that S revised the second version in order to make it seem more like a translation and to show his willingness to acknowledge his source. See 255.

(257)

Johnstone, J. E., "The Classical Element in Shakespeare." See 16.

Ecclesiazusae was the source of *1H4,* II, iv, 367 ff. ("when I was about thy years, Hal . . .").

(258)

Rechner, Leonhard, *Aristophanes in England: eine literarhistorische Untersuchung,* Frankfort on Main, 1914, p. 38.

S did not read Aristophanes' works.

(259)

Robertson, J. M., *The Baconian Heresy,* p. 241. See 18.

There is no justification for suggesting that *Tem,* IV, i, 116 ("Scarcity and want shall shun you") was dependent upon a passage in *Plutus.*

(260)

Theobald, William, *The Classical Element in the Shakespeare Plays,* pp. 78-82. See 9.

About a dozen Sn passages are cited which were dependent upon Aristophanes' plays.

Aristotle

During the fifteenth and sixteenth centuries, Aristotle's works were frequently translated into Latin, English, and the modern European languages. These translations are not listed here since no source commentary between 1904 and 1940 has been found which suggests S's direct use of an accurate text of Aristotle.

(261)

Campbell, L. B., "A Note for Baconians," *MLN*, 53 (1938) : 21-23.

In *TC*, II, ii, 163-171 ("Paris and Troilus, you have both said well . . .") S erroneously cited Aristotle as an authority. The fact that Bacon's *Advancement of Learning* contains this error has proved grist for the Baconian mill, but the same error also occurs in Grimald's address which prefixes his translation of Cicero's *Thre Bokes of Duties*. Either Grimald or some incorrect Latin edition of Aristotle, unnoticed until now, was S's source.

(262)

Sandys, J. E., "Scholarship" in *Shakespeare's England*, p. 268. See 12.

There is little evidence to substantiate the claim that S was acquainted with the works of Aristotle. His erroneous use of Aristotle's name in *TC*, II, ii, 166, is not to be explained by identifying S with Bacon but by the fact that both S and Bacon depended upon a colloquy of Erasmus.

(263)

Theobald, William, *The Classical Element in the Shakespeare Plays*, pp. 82-84. See 9.

Passages from several Sn plays are cited to demonstrate the influence of Aristotelian doctrine on S. *TC*, II, ii, 163 ff. ("Paris and Troilus, . . .") was probably suggested to S by a passage in Erasmus' *Colloquies*, which was derived from *Nichomachean Ethics*.

See also 45.

Athenaeus

LATIN: *Dipnosophistarum sive coenae sapientum libri XV*, tr. N. Comes, Venice, 1556.

. . . *Dipnosophistarum libri quindecim*, tr. Jacobus Dalechampius, Lyons, 1583.

(264)

Johnstone, J. E., "The Classical Element in Shakespeare." See 16.

The "feast of languages" conceit (*LLL*, V, i, 39 ff.) was derived from an anecdote about Aeschylus which Athenaeus recorded.

(265)

McCartney, E. S., "A Possible Indebtedness of Shakespeare to Athenaeus," *Classical J*, 24 (1928): 213-214.

In *LLL*, V, i, 39-43 ("They have been at a great feast of languages . . .") S probably borrowed from Athenaeus VIII, 347 E. A similar concept is to be found in *MA*, II, iii, 19 ff. ("He was wont to speak plain . . .").

(266)

Theobald, William, *The Classical Element in the Shakespeare Plays*, pp. 85-86. See 9.

TC, II, iii, 260 ff. ("and, for thy vigour, Bull-bearing Milo . . .") resembles some lines of Dorieus quoted by Athenaeus, X, 1, 2.

Aurelius Antoninus, Marcus [Not to be confused with Marcus Aurelius Antoninus, pseudonym of Antonius de Guevara.]

GREEK AND LATIN: *De seipso seu vita sua libri XII, Guilielmo Xylandro interprete*, Zurich, 1559.

FRENCH: *Institution de la vie humaine*, tr. Pardoux Du Prat, Lyons, 1570.

(267)

"Editorial," *Baconiana*, 24 (1939): 3.

Aurelius' works were not translated into English until after S's death and were difficult to obtain in the original in England. In the churchyard scene, however, Hamlet's thoughts on Alexander the Great suggest the influence of similar allusions to Alexander in Aurelius' *Meditations*, VI. *KL*, V, ii, 9 ff. ("Men must endure their going hence, even as their coming hither: Ripeness is all") is suggestive of *Meditations*, IV, 48.

(268)

Johnstone, J. E., "The Classical Element in Shakespeare." See 16.

H, II, ii, 259 ff. ("there is nothing either good or bad, but thinking makes it so") was derived either from Marcus Aurelius Antoninus or from Heraclitus.

(269)

Theobald, William, *The Classical Element in the Shakespeare Plays,* pp. 71-73. See 9.

Passages in *H, 2H4,* and *Mac* show the influence of Aurelius.

Cassius Cocceianus, Dio

GREEK AND LATIN: *Romanorum historiarum libri XXV,* tr. Guilielmus Xylander [Paris], 1592.

ITALIAN: *De fatti de' Romani dalla guerra di Candia,* tr. from the Latin of Xylander by F. Baldelli, Venice, 1585.

See 30.

Dictys

LATIN: *De bello trojano,* Lyons, 1520.

ENGLISH: *The Auncient Historie and Onely Trewe and Syncere Cronicle of the Warres betwixte the Grecians and the Troyans . . . written by Daretus a Troyan and Dictus a Grecian,* tr. John Lydgate, London, 1555.

According to tradition, the Latin version was translated from the Greek by Quintus Septimius.

For Lydgate's *Troy Book* as a source of *TC,* see **Colonne, Guido Delle**

(270)

Thelemann, Anna, "Dictys als Mitquelle von Shakespeares *Troilus,*" *Ar,* 133 (1915) : 91-96.

S obtained Dictys' version of the Troilus and Cressida story either indirectly through Dekker and Chettle's drama on the subject or through a French version of Dictys by De la Lande, Paris, 1556. A detailed listing of parallels is offered to show S's indebtedness not only to the contents of the Dictys version but also to the additions written by the French translator.

(271)

Theobald, William, *The Classical Element in the Shakespeare Plays,* pp. 150-151. See 9.

TC, V, viii, 2-8 ("Thy goodly armour thus hath cost thy life . . .") was suggested by Dictys Cretensis, III, 15.

Dio Cassius, see Cassius Cocceianus, Dio

Diodorus Siculus

During the sixteenth century, the work of Diodorus Siculus was frequently translated into Latin and into the modern tongues. However, because of Joseph de Perott's marked hesitancy in suggesting this history as a Sn source, the translations of Siculus are not recorded here.

(272)

Perott, Joseph de, "Shakespeare and Diodorus Siculus," *Classical J*, 18 (1923): 571.

There is a "mere possibility" that a reading of Diodorus Siculus, XII, 13, suggested to S *MA*, III, iii, 14 ("to be a well-favoured man is the gift of fortune; but to write and read comes by nature").

Euripides

LATIN AND GREEK-AND-LATIN: *Tragoediae XVIII . . . Dorotheo Camillo interprete,* Basel, 1550. [According to F. A. Ebert, the translator's real name was Rdf. Collinus.]

Euripides in Latinum sermonem conversus, tr. G. Stiblinus, Basel, 1562.

Tragoediae, tr. Philip Melancthon, preface by Guilielmus Xylander, Frankfort, 1562.

Tragoediae selectae Aeschyli, Sophoclis, Euripidis [tr. Erasmus, Buchanan, *et al.,* no pl.], 1567.

Ιραγῳδίαι ιθ' . . . *Tragoediae XIX,* tr. Gulielmus [*sic*] Canterus, Antwerp, 1580.

Tragoediae XIX, tr. M. Aemilius Portus, Heidelberg, 1597.

'Αριστόλόγια Εὐριπίδειη . . . *Aristologia Euripidea,* compiled by Michael Neander, Basel, 1559.

. . . *Tres tragoediae, Phoenissae, Hippolytus coronatus, atque Andromacha,* tr. G. Ratallerus, Antwerp, 1581.

Q. Sept. Florentis Christiani Andromacha, Leyden, 1594.

Cyclops, tr. Q. S. F. Christianus, Paris, 1605.

Cyclops [two Latin versions, one by Melancthon, the other by C. Martianus], Strassburg, 1582.

Phoenissae, tr. G. Calaminus, Strassburg, 1577.

FRENCH: *La Tragédie . . . nommee Hecuba* [tr. L. de Baïf], Paris, 1550.

Hecuba, tr. Guillaume Bouchetel, Paris, 1550.

L'Iphigène [tr. Thomas Sibilet], Paris, 1549.

ITALIAN: *Alceste,* tr. Geronimo Giustiniano, Genoa, 1599.

L'Hecuba, tr. G. Balcianelli, Verona, 1592.

Tragedie di M. L. Dolce: Giocasta [from *Phoenissae* of Euripides], *Medea* [from Euripides], *Didone, Ifigenia* [from Euripides], *Thieste* [from Seneca], *Hecuba* [from Euripides] ; Venice, 1560.

ENGLISH: *Jocasta,* tr. from *Phoenissae* by George Gascoigne and F. Kinwelmershe, printed in *A Hundreth Sundrie Flowres of George Gascoigne,* London [1572].

The general tendency of such modern critics as E. E. Stoll and Gilbert Murray is to deny Euripidean influence in *H.*

(273)

Barker, Ernest, "A Shakespeare Discovery," *Spectator,* 158 (1937) : 615-616.

Ulysses' speech on degree (*TC,* I, iii, 78 ff.) was derived not from Euripides but from Elyot's *The Boke Named the Governour,* 1 and 2.

(274)

Johnstone, J. E., "The Classical Element in Shakespeare." See 16.

From Euripides, S derived *R2,* I, iii, 213 ("How long a time lies in one little word") ; and *1H4,* V, iv, 120 ("The better part of valour is discretion"). See also 75.

(275)

Lucas, F. L., *Euripides and His Influence,* Boston, 1923, pp. 107-110.

Various suggestions of Sn indebtedness to Euripides are considered but discarded. Of these, the most plausible is that *1H4,* I, iii, 201-205 ("By heaven methinks it were an easy leap . . .") was derived from *Phoenissae,* 504-506 ("I'd go where rise the stars . . ."). Even if S was here dependent upon *Phoenissae,* it is not necessary to conclude that he was familiar with the Greek of Euripides. He might have obtained the idea indirectly from Gascoigne's translation, *Jocasta.* He also might have obtained the idea from a translation of Plutarch's *On Brotherly Love.*

(276)

Robertson, J. M., *Did Shakespeare Write Titus Andronicus? A Study in Elizabethan Literature,* London, 1905, pp. 225-227.

In an attempt to disprove S's authorship of *Titus,* Euripides' *Hecuba* is given as the source of *Titus,* I, i, 136 ff. ("The self-same gods, that arm'd the Queen of Troy . . .").

(277)

Theobald, William, *The Classical Element in the Shakespeare Plays,* pp. 156-163. See 9.

Over a score of Sn passages are cited which might have been influenced by Euripidean dramas.

See also 26 and 310.

Heliodorus

ENGLISH: *An Aethiopian Historie,* tr. T. Underdowne, London, 1587. "The Beginning of Heliodorus His Aethiopical History," tr. A. Fraunce in *The Countesse of Pembrokes Yvychurche,* London, 1591.

Several lists of S's reading include *An Aethiopian History,* without discussing S's specific indebtedness to the work.

(278)

[Cowl, R. P.] *Sources of the Text of Henry the Fourth,* pp. 42-43. See 15.

2H4, IV, v, 81-86 ("I found the prince . . .") and *1H4,* IV, i, 113 ("They come like sacrifices . . .") were derived from Heliodorus' *Aethiopica.*

(279)

Sandys, J. E., "Scholarship" in *Shakespeare's England,* p. 270. See 12.

The reference to the Egyptian thief (*TN,* V, i, 121-123) was intended as an allusion to Heliodorus' *Aethiopian History,* translated by Abraham Fraunce.

Hesiod

LATIN AND GREEK-AND-LATIN: *Duo libri georgicon . . . opera et dies,* tr. M. Planudes, ed. O. Nachtigall, Strassburg [1515].
. . . *Opera,* tr. Ulpius Franekerensis, N. Valle, Boninus Mombritius, *et al.,* Basel [1542].
Utilis . . . liber . . . opera et dies, tr. J. Brixius, Lyons, 1550.
Poema . . . opera et dies, tr. Joannes Frisius, Zurich, 1562.

FRENCH: *Les Livres* . . . *intitulez les œuvres et les jours,* tr. Richard le Blanc, Lyons, 1547.

Les Trois Livres . . . *appelez les œuvres et les jours,* tr. Lambert d'Aneau [Paris], 1571.

Les Besognes [*sic* in Lanson] *et jours,* tr. J.-A. de Baïf in *Etrenes de poësie française,* Paris, 1574.

Les Besongnes et les jours, tr. Jaques le Gras, Paris, 1586.

(280)

Krappe, A. H., "Shakespeare Notes," pp. 180-182. See 34.

Hesiod's *Works and Days,* 705, was the source of *H,* I, iii, 58 ff. ("And these few precepts . . ."). Although Hesiod was not translated into English until 1618, Latin, Italian, and French versions were in existence when *H* was written. [This bibliographer was unable to find any translations of Hesiod into Italian which were in print prior to S's *H.*]

See also 86.

Homer

LATIN AND GREEK-AND-LATIN: *Iliados epitome per Pindarum Thebanum* [Poitiers, 1495].

Ilias, tr. N. de Valle, Cologne [1522].

Tres orationes in triplici dicendi genere ex Homeri, tr. Leonardus Aretinus, Nuremberg, 1523.

Ilias, tr. Andreas Divus Justinopolitanus, Venice [1537].

Ilias, tr. Helius Eobanus Hessus, Basel, 1540.

Omnia quae quidam [*sic*] *extant opera* [tr. several hands], Basel, 1551.

Opera, tr. Sebastian Castalio, Basel, 1561.

Belli Trojani scriptores . . . *Homerus* [tr. V. Obsopaeus, N. de Valle, H. Eobanus Hessus], ed. Georg Henisch, Basel, 1573.

Poemata duo [tr. E. Hodeniccius, Paris], 1578.

Opera, partly revised by Henricus Stephanus [no pl.], 1588.

FRENCH: *Les Iliades,* tr. Jehan Samxon, Paris, 1530.

Le Quatorziesme Livre de l'Iliade, tr. Antoine de Cotel, Paris, 1578.

Les XXIV Livres de l'Iliade, tr. Hugues Salel and Amadis Jamyn, Paris, 1584. [Portions of this work were published earlier.]

ITALIAN: *Il primo libro de la Iliade,* tr. Francesco Gussano, Venice, 1544.

L'Iliade [I-V], tr. Paolo La Badessa, Padua, 1564.

Il primo libro della Iliade, tr. Luigi Groto Cieco d'Hadria, Venice, 1570.

L'Achille et l'Enea [abridged edition], tr. Lodovico Dolce, Venice, 1571.

L'Ulisse, tr. Lodovico Dolce, Venice, 1573.

ENGLISH: *Ten Books of Homers Iliades,* tr. from French by A. Hall, London, 1581.

Achilles Shield [from *Iliad*], tr. G. Chapman, London, 1598.

Seaven Bookes of the Iliades, tr. G. Chapman, London, 1598.

Homer . . . Twelve Bookes of His Iliads, tr. G. Chapman, London [1610?].

(281)

Brooke, Tucker, "Shakespeare's Study in Culture and Anarchy," *Yale R,* 17 (1928) : 571-577.

Some of the difficulties in interpreting *TC* arise from the fact that S superimposed upon his main source (Chaucer) conflicting concepts which he derived from Caxton's *Troy Book* and from Chapman's Homer.

(282)

Haynes, French, "Shakespeare and the Troy Story." See 117.

Although it is deemed of less importance as a source than Caxton, Homer's influence on *TC* is analyzed in detail.

(283)

Henderson, W. B. D., "Shakespeare's *Troilus and Cressida* Yet Deeper in Its Tradition." See 37.

In writing *TC,* S unquestionably depended upon Chaucer, Caxton, Lydgate, and upon Chapman's *Seaven Bookes of the Iliades.*

(284)

Keller, Wolfgang, "Shakespeares *Troilus und Cressida,*" pp. 190-191. See 38.

J. S. P. Tatlock [see 290 and 291] is justified in discarding Chapman's translation of Homer as the source of *TC.* Instead, S probably used Caxton as his source. See also 119.

(285)

Lawrence, W. W., *Shakespeare's Problem Comedies,* pp. 155-157. See 55.

J. S. P. Tatlock's conclusions regarding the source of *TC* are correct. See 290 and 291.

(286)

Robertson, J. M., *The Baconian Heresy,* pp. 215, 241. See 18.

Neither Pandarus' comments on the Greek warriors, nor Hamlet's "large discourse" (*H,* IV, iv, 36), nor Iris' reference to the "pole-clipt vineyard" (*Tem,* IV, i, 68) was derived from the *Iliad.*

(287)

Rollins, H. E., "The Troilus-Cressida Story from Chaucer to Shakespeare," *PMLA,* 32 (1917) : 382-429.

This detailed article supports J. S. P. Tatlock's opinions regarding the source of *TC* [see 290 and 291] and traces the development of the Troilus-Cressida story in English literature.

(288)

Royster, J. F., "*Richard III,* IV, 4 and the Three Marys of the Mediaeval Drama," *MLN,* 25 (1910) : 173-174.

The Iliad, XXIV, is the closest classical parallel to *R3,* IV, iv. A still closer parallel, however, is to be found in the *planctus* of the three Marys in medieval Resurrection dramas.

(289)

Scott, J. A., "An Unnoticed Homeric Phrase in Shakespeare," *Classical Philology,* 33 (1938) : 414.

Zeus' "I grant thee willingly though against my will" (Chapman's Homer, IV) was the source of *Cor,* IV, vi, 145-146 ("though we willingly consented to his banishment, yet it was against our will").

(290)

Tatlock, J. S. P., "The Chief Problem in Shakespeare," *Sewanee R,* 24 (1916) : 129-147.

The chief source of *TC* was, probably, Caxton. Another source was Chaucer's *Troilus and Criseyde.* If S used Homer's *Iliad* at all, he obtained it in some translation other than Chapman's. Perhaps S found all this material in an old English play, which is no longer extant, rather than in Caxton, Chaucer, and Homer. See 284, 285, and 287.

(291)

Tatlock, J. S. P., "The Siege of Troy in Elizabethan Literature, Especially in Shakespeare and Heywood," *PMLA,* 30 (1915) : 673-770.

TC was not based upon Chapman's Homer. This is proved by the fact that the play was written before Chapman translated some of the Iliadic material which S used in this drama. S might have depended upon some French, Latin, or Greek-and-Latin version of the *Iliad*. Since, however, no other Sn play was definitely influenced by the *Iliad*, one may assume that the Homeric influence in *TC* was derived indirectly from an English play, now lost, upon which Heywood's *Iron Age* also depended. See 284, 285, and 287.

(292)

Theobald, William, *The Classical Element in the Shakespeare Plays,* pp. 180-208. See 9.

Passages in over a score of Sn plays are cited which might have been influenced by Homer.

See also 305 and 317.

Lucianus

LATIN AND GREEK-AND-LATIN: *Dialogi VI,* tr. Rinuccio Aret. and Joh. Aurispa [Rome, 1470].

. . . θεων διαλογοι . . . *Deorum dialogi* [tr. O. Nachtigall], Strassburg, 1515.

. . . *Dialogi duo Charon et Tyrannus,* tr. Petrus Mosellanus Protegensis, The Hague, 1518.

Dialogi aliquot, tr. D. Erasmus and Nicolas Buscoducensis, Antwerp, 1528.

Dialogi aliquot, tr. N. Grudius, H. Marius, and J. Scd'm, Strassburg, 1529.

Opera quae quidem extant omnia, tr. Jacobus Micyllus, *et al.,* Lyons, 1549.

Dialogi coelestes, marini, et inferni . . . *editi in usum puerorum* [no tr.], Basel, 1550.

Dialogi selecti, tr. Johannes Sambucus, Strassburg, 1554.

Timon, tr. Johannes Sambucus, Strassburg, 1550.

Since many of the Latin editions of the *Dialogues* (published before and within S's lifetime) lack the translator's name, the above list is, necessarily, incomplete. It may be well to note further that many of the Latin translations listed above were frequently republished during the sixteenth and early seventeenth centuries. These facts testify to the popularity of Lucian's works during the Renaissance.

FRENCH: *Trente dialogues,* tr. Geofroy Tory, Paris, 1529.

Les Oeuvres, tr. Filbert Bretin, Paris, 1583.

Le Menteur, tr. Louis Meigret, Paris, 1548.

[A Dialogue in] *Poësie d'Estienne Forcadel,* Lyons, 1551.

ITALIAN: *I dialogi,* tr. Nicolò da Lonigo, Venice, 1541.

Due dialoghi, tr. L. Domenichi, Florence, 1548.

Timone comoedia by Matteo Maria Boiardo, tr. from Lucian [no pl.], 1500.

SPANISH: *Dialogos* [tr. Pedro Simon Abril?], León, 1550.

El dialogo . . . de Icaro-Menippo, tr. Ioannes de Jarava [no pl.], 1546.

GERMAN: *Spiegel der menschlichen blödigkeit . . . Drei schöner Gesprech des Tichters Luciani,* tr. J. Vielfeldt, Strassburg, 1545.

Von Klaffern "Hernach volgen zway Puechlein das ain Lucianus . . .," tr. Dietrich von Pleningen, Landsshüt, 1516.

Timon oder Leuthas, tr. Jac. Schenck, Worms, 1530.

ENGLISH: [*Necromantia*] *A Dialogue of the Poet Lucyan* [tr. Rastell? London? 1530?].

A Dialogue betwene Lucian and Diogenes [tr. T. Eliot, London, n.d.]. See also Introduction, footnote 5.

(293)

Blake, H. M., *Classic Myth in the Poetic Drama of the Age of Elizabeth,* pp. 15-17. See 101.

Although there are resemblances between *Timon* and Lucian's *Dialogues,* Lucian was not available to S in English nor is there any reason to believe that S could have read the Greek version.

(294)

Fox, W. S., "Lucian in the Grave Scene of *Hamlet,*" *PQ,* 2 (1923): 132-141.

Striking parallels between the graveyard scene in *H* (V, i) and Lucian's *Charon, Menippus,* and *Dialogues of the Dead* testify to S's dependence upon Lucian.

(295)

Fox, W. S., "Sources of the Grave Scene in *Hamlet,*" *Transactions of the Royal Society of Canada,* Third Series, 17 (1923), Section 2, pp. 71-80.

This is a preliminary article on the possible sources of the graveyard scene in *H*. Elements of the graveyard scene to be found in the usually accepted *H* sources are noted. Stress is laid on the Lucianic quality of Hamlet's discourse on skulls, and a survey is made of the versions of Lucian available to S. S did not read Lucian in the original Greek but might have obtained some Latin or English translation.

(296)

Gray, Arthur, *"The Comedy of Errors."* See 114.

S borrowed some incidents of *Timon* from Lucian's *Dialogues*, and from the name of its author he might have derived the name of Luciana used in *CE*.

(297)

Review: Keller, Wolfgang, *"The Authorship of Timon of Athens* by Ernest Hunter Wright . . . ," *SJ*, 47 (1911): 296-298.

Despite E. H. Wright to the contrary [see 342], Lucian's *Dialogue of Timon* influenced S's *Timon*, I, i, 143 ff. ("This gentleman of mine hath serv'd me long . . .") and *Timon*, V, i, 1-112.

(298)

Krappe, A. H., "Shakespeare Notes," pp. 178-180. See 34.

The comparison of men to actors performing on a stage (*Mac*, V, v, 23-28) was derived from a translation of the following passage in Lucian's *Menippus:* "The life of man came before me under the likeness of a great pageant. . . ."

(299)

Theobald, William, *The Classical Element in the Shakespeare Plays*, pp. 241-243. See 9.

Lines in *H, Cor, JC, Mac*, and *O* are cited which might have been dependent upon Lucian.

See also 338, 339, 340, 342, and 452.

Marianus

During the sixteenth century several Latin and French translations were published of selections from the *Anthologia Palatina*. Since they were unavailable for examination, it could not be determined which of them include Marianus' epigrams. According to Edward Dowden, *The Sonnets of William Shakspere*, London, 1881, pp. 249-250, they were published in Latin in *Selecta epigrammata*, ed. J. Cornarius, Basel, 1529. See also 301 and 302.

(300)

Greenwood, G. G., *Is There a Shakespeare Problem?* p. 151. See 64.

S's last two sonnets were dependent upon Marianus, whose epigrams S might have read either in Greek or in a Latin translation.

(301)

Hegedüs, Stephan v., "Die griechische Quelle zu Shakespeares zwei letzten Sonetten," *Ungarische Rundschau*, 2 (1913): 586-596.

There is remarkable parallelism between the last two sonnets of S and Marianus. Fourteen of Marianus' epigrams were translated by a supposed "Zenodotos" into Latin and were frequently included in Latin anthologies of the sixteenth century. S might somehow have obtained this Latin version in manuscript form.

(302)

Wolff, M. J., "Zu den Sonetten," *SJ*, 47 (1911): 191-192.

S might have read Marianus' epigram, which influenced sonnets 153-154, not only in the Latin but also in the Italian. It is to be found in *Versi et regole della nuova poesta toscana* of Claudio Tolomei, Rome, 1539, signature M IIII.

Plato

LATIN AND GREEK-AND-LATIN: *Omnia . . . opera*, tr. M. Ficinus, Basel, 1546.
. . . *Opera*, tr. J. Cornarius, Basel, 1561.
απαντα τα σωζομενα . . . *Opera quae extant omnia*, tr. J. Serranus [ed. H. Estienne], Paris, 1578.
Dialogi, tr. Bilibaldus Pirckheymerus, Nuremberg, 1523.
Dialogi sex, tr. Sb. Corradus, Lyons, 1543.
Apologia Socratis, tr. Leonardus Aretinus [no pl., c. 1472].
Timaeus . . . interprete M. Tullio Cicerone et Chalcidio, Paris, 1578.

FRENCH: *L'Apologie de Socrate*, tr. F. Hotman, Lyons, 1549.
Le Dialogue intitulé Io, tr. R. le Blanc, Paris, 1546.
Le Phedon, tr. Loys le Roy, Paris, 1559.
La République, tr. L. le Roy, Paris, 1600. [Portions of this work were published earlier.]
Le Banquet [*Symposium*], tr. Maturin Heret, Paris, 1556.
Le Sympose, tr. Loys le Roy, Paris, 1559.
Discours de l'honneste amour [*Le Banquet*], tr. Guy le Fevre de la Boderie [no pl.], 1578.

Timée, tr. Louis le Roy, Paris, 1552.

ITALIAN: *Tutte le opere,* tr. Dardi Bembo, Venice, 1601.

I dialoghi, tr. M. Sebastiano Erizzo, Venice, 1574.

Il Fedro, tr. F. Figliucci, Rome, 1544.

La republica, tr. Pamphilo Fiorimbene, Venice, 1554.

For Proclus' commentary, see **Proclus.**

(303)

Anders, Heinrich, "Randglossen zu *Shakespeare's Belesenheit."* See 248.

S's concept of the poet's frenzy (*MND,* V, i, 12 ff.) is to be found in Plato's *Phaedrus, Ion,* and *Symposium.*

(304)

Burnet, John, "Shakespeare and Greek Philosophy," *Essays and Addresses* with a memoir by Lord Charnwood, London, 1929, pp. 163-168.

Although *MV,* V, i, 58 ff. ("Sit Jessica . . .") clearly expresses the Pythagorean doctrine that is found in Plato's *Timaeus,* S obtained his knowledge of Plato indirectly through such medieval channels as the moralities and interludes.

(305)

Hanford, J. H., "A Platonic Passage in Shakespeare's *Troilus and Cressida," SP,* 13 (1916): 100-109.

There is no incontrovertible proof of direct Platonic influence on S, but the philosophy of degree expounded in *H5,* I, ii, 178-213 ("While that the armed hand . . .") and *TC,* I, iii, 78-137 ("The specialty of rule hath been neglected . . .") suggests such an influence. S might have read Plato's *Dialogues* in Latin or Italian. *The Republic* was also translated into French. S might have been stimulated to dip into Homer and Plato in order to obtain the correct tone for his Greek drama of *TC.*

(306)

Johnstone, J. E., "The Classical Element in Shakespeare." See 16.

Plato is suggested as one of the possible sources from which S obtained his knowledge regarding the circulation of the blood and from which he obtained the comparison in *R2,* III, iv, 55 ff. ("O! what a pity is it . . .").

(307)

Kranz, Walther, "Shakespeare und die Antike," *ESn,* 73 (1938-1939): 32-38.

No satisfactory explanation has been found for the existence of Platonic concepts in *MV*, V, i, 58 ff. ("Sit, Jessica . . .") ; *JC*, I, ii, 52 ("the eye sees not itself") ; and *TC*, III, iii, 107 ff. ("eye to eye opposed . . .").

(308)

Robertson, J. M., *The Baconian Heresy*, pp. 183-189, 203-204, 247. See 18.

Despite claims to the contrary, the following passages were not derived from Plato: *TC*, III, iii, 105 ff. ("nor doth the eye . . .") ; *1H6*, I, vi, 6-7 ("Thy promises are like Adonis' gardens . . .") ; *H5*, I, ii, 183 ff. ("Therefore doth heaven divide . . .") ; and *H*, III, i, 56 ff. ("To be, or not to be . . .").

(309)

Sandys, J. E., "Scholarship" in *Shakespeare's England*, pp. 267-268. See 12.

Plato's *First Alcibiades* may be discarded as a possible source of *TC*, III, iii, 95 ff. ("A strange fellow here Writes me . . .").

(310)

Stronach, George, "Shakespeare's Scholarship." See 72.

Through Latin translation, S became acquainted not only with the principal tragedies of Sophocles, Aeschylus, and Euripides, but also with Plato's *Alcibiades* and *Republic*, as J. C. Collins has suggested. See 72 n.

(311)

Theobald, William, *The Classical Element in the Shakespeare Plays*, pp. 297-302. See 9.

Plato was the source of passages in half a dozen Sn plays.

Plutarch

ENGLISH: *The Lives of the Noble Grecians and Romanes,* tr. T. North, London, 1579; 1595; 1603.

William Painter, *The Palace of Pleasure,* London, 1566, I, xxvii, xxviii and II, iii.

The Amorous and Tragicall Tales (Sentences out of the Greeke Philosophers) by J. Sanford [no pl.], 1567.

A Righte Noble and Pleasant History of the Successors of Alexander Surnamed the Great, taken out of Diodorus Siculus . . . and Plutarch, tr. T. Stocker, London, 1569.

The Education or Bringinge Up of Children, tr. T. Elyot, London, [1535?].

Howe One May Take Profite of His Enmyes [tr. T. Elyot], London, [1535?].

A President for Parentes, Teaching the Vertuous Training Up of Children and Holesome Information of Young Men, tr. and augmented by Ed. Grant, London, 1571.

Three Morall Treatises: The Learned Prince, The Fruites of Foes, The Port of Rest, tr. T. Blundville, London, 1580.

A Philosophical Treatise Concerning the Quietness of the Mind, tr. J. Clapham [no pl.], 1589.

The Philosophie Commonly Called the Morals, tr. Philemon Holland, London, 1603.

THE INFLUENCE OF PLUTARCH'S *Lives* ON *JC, AC,* AND *Cor*

(312)

Altkamp, Ingeborg, *Die Gestaltung Caesars bei Plutarch und Shakespeare,* Würzburg, 1933, 70 pp.

In writing *JC,* S followed Plutarch closely but not slavishly. S's deviations from his source enhance the impression of reality.

(313)

Ayres, H. M., "Shakespeare's *Julius Caesar* in the Light of Some Other Versions," *PMLA,* 25 (1910): 183-227.

S's Caesar retains the stoicism depicted in Plutarch. The additional characteristics of pomposity and human infirmity found in S's characterization were derived from pseudo-Senecan Caesar plays.

(314)

Benetta, Sister Mary, *Caesar in Plutarch and in Shakespeare,* MS Thesis, American Catholic U, Washington, D. C., 1924, 23 pp.

In writing *JC,* S followed Plutarch closely. The drama is considered scene by scene in relation to this source.

(315)

Brooke, C. F. T., ed., *Shakespeare's Plutarch,* New York, London, 1909, 2 vols.

A brief discussion of S's indebtedness to Plutarch in *JC* is followed by the text of Plutarch's "Life of Julius Caesar" and "Life of Marcus Brutus." The passages upon which S depended are marked with an asterisk. In volume II, the same procedure is used to demonstrate S's dependence upon Plutarch in *Cor* and *AC.*

(316)

Büttner, Richard, "Zu *Coriolan* und seiner Quelle," *SJ*, 41 (1905) : 45-53.

Several slight deviations from Plutarch's "Life of Coriolanus" in S's play of that name might have been caused by errors in North's translation, by S's use of North's marginal notes, and by S's use of some suggestions from other biographies in the North collection. S intensified the heroic quality of his hero, Coriolanus.

(317)

Draper, J. W., "The Realism of Shakespeare's Roman Plays." See 169.

The local coloring in S's Roman plays was not derived solely from Plutarch. S attempted to enhance the realism of *Cor,* for example, by the use of some suggestions from Ovid. He might have obtained hints for Antony's description of the agriculture near the Nile from Leo Africanus. He borrowed some details for *AC* from Homer as well as obtaining a number of additional hints from English writers and English customs.

(318)

Ellehauge, Martin, "The Use of His Sources Made by Shakespeare in *Julius Caesar* and *Antony and Cleopatra,*" *ESn,* 65 (1931) : 197-210.

The influence of Plutarch on *JC* and *AC* is carefully analyzed. Although Plutarch is their main source, some of the concepts and some of the wording in these plays suggest the influence of earlier English dramas, especially of Daniel's *Cleopatra.*

(319)

Fisher, L. A., "Shakspere and the Capitol," *MLN,* 22 (1907) : 177-182.

S's setting Caesar's murder in the Capitol (*JC,* III, i) need not necessarily be considered a deliberate deviation from Plutarch. S might have thought the words "Capitol"and "Senate" synonymous. Medieval references to Caesar's having been killed in the Capitol are cited. Polonius' statement that he acted the part of Caesar who "was killed i' the capitol" (*H,* III, ii, 109-110) suggests that S might have obtained the concept from a university play.

(320)

Genouy, Hector, "Tradition romaine et *Julius Caesar* de Shakespeare," *Revue de l'enseignement des langues vivantes,* 48 (1931) : 201-216, 241-254.

A detailed comparison of *JC* and Plutarch's *Lives* demonstrates that, despite his historical inaccuracies, S portrayed the Roman tradition more vividly and more truly than Plutarch did.

(321)

Heuer, Hermann, "Shakespeare und Plutarch: Studien zu Wertwelt und Lebensgefühl im *Coriolanus*," *A*, 62 (1938) : 321-346.

In order to appreciate S's method of transforming his sources, a detailed comparative study is made of Volumnia's plea in *Cor*, V, iii, and its source, North's Plutarch.

(322)

Hirzel, Rudolf, *Plutarch*, Leipzig, 1912, pp. 140-145.

Some specific details in S's Roman plays are analyzed to demonstrate S's masterly manipulation of Plutarch as a source. Examples are also given of S's indebtedness to Plutarch for minor suggestions in other plays.

(323)

Keller, Wolfgang, "Zwei Bemerkungen zu *Julius Caesar*," *SJ*, 45 (1909) : 219-228.

Specific passages in *JC* are noted which demonstrate S's close adherence to Plutarch as a source.

(324)

Linscheid, John Edward, *Coriolanus: A Study in Relation to Its Source*, MS Thesis, Graduate College of the State U of Iowa, 1929, 167 pp.

S's deviations from Plutarch in *Cor* are considered in detail, act by act, and character by character.

(325)

MacCallum, M. W., *Shakespeare's Roman Plays, passim.* See 253.

The influence of Plutarch's *Lives* on *JC, AC,* and *Cor* is analyzed in careful detail. Minor influences of Plutarch on other Sn works are alluded to *passim.* See also 253.

(326)

Meinck, Carl, *Über das örtliche und zeitliche Kolorit in Shakespeares Römerdramen und Ben Jonsons Catiline (Studien zur Englischen Philologie, 38)*, Halle a. S., 1910, *passim.*

In order to throw light on S's use of local coloring in the Roman plays, his use of and his deviations from North's Plutarch are considered incidentally.

(327)

Morsbach, Lorenz, *Shakespeares Cäsarbild* (*Studien zur Englischen Philologie*, 88), Halle a. S., 1935, 32 pp.

Although Plutarch was S's chief source for *JC*, in his creation of the character of Caesar, S's divergence from his source is of great significance.

(328)

Murry, J. M., "North's Plutarch," *Countries of the Mind*, Series II, London, 1931, pp. 78-96.

S's characterization of Julius Caesar and the colorfulness of his portrayal of Antony and Cleopatra are to be explained not by his personal reactions but by his dependence upon North's Plutarch.

(329)

Review: "North's Plutarch," *TLS*, September 12, 1929, pp. 689-690.

It was not only for the plot but also for the atmosphere of *JC, AC,* and *Cor* that S was dependent upon Plutarch.

(330)

Robertson, J. M., *The Baconian Heresy*, pp. 191-192. See 18.

That S in his Roman plays used North's Plutarch is accepted unquestionably. S made the same errors as those found in North and added a few additional errors of his own as well.

(331)

Sandys, J. E., "Scholarship" in *Shakespeare's England*, pp. 269-270. See 12.

S did not obtain the funeral oration of Antony in *JC* from North's Plutarch, but from that source he obtained the "I came, saw, and overcame" of *LLL*, IV, i, 70 and *2H4*, IV, iii, 46.

(332)

Sarrazin, G., "Shakespeare und Orlando Pescetti," *ESn*, 46 (1912-1913): 347-354.

Although Plutarch was the chief source of *JC*, S was also influenced by Pescetti when he wrote *JC*, II and III. Parallels between Pescetti and *JC* are listed in detail. No translation of Pescetti written during the Sn period is now extant, but it is possible that such a translation existed.

(333)

Schücking, L. L., *Character Problems in Shakespeare's Plays*, London, 1922, pp. 39-50, 120-144.

In the early portion of *AC,* S's heroine is not so great a figure as she is in Plutarch, but in the second half of the drama, Cleopatra is more dominant than in S's source.

S should not be charged with having transformed Caesar into a weakling since he adhered closely to Plutarch and to Renaissance tradition.

(334)

Schütze, Johannes, "Daniels *Cleopatra* und Shakespeare," *ESn,* 71 (1936): 58-72.

The literary connections between S's *AC* and Daniel's *Cleopatra* occur only because both were dependent upon Plutarch.

(335)

Shackford, M. H., *Plutarch in Renaissance England with Special Reference to Shakespeare* [no pl.], 1929, S sources: pp. 35-40.

Plutarch's *Lives* was the main source of *JC, AC, Cor,* and *Timon* and also supplied S with suggestions which he used in over a half dozen other Sn plays. No categorical statement can be made regarding the influence of Plutarch's *Morals* on S. Plutarch's *Of Exile or Banishment* in the Holland translation might, perhaps, have influenced the speeches of Belarius on exile (*Cym,* III, iii) and several concepts in *Tem.*

Shakespeare's Plutarch, see 315.

(336)

Sonnenschein, E. A., "Shakspere and Stoicism." See 29.

In *JC,* S showed a clear understanding of the Roman outlook on life. His difficulties in explaining Brutus' attitude toward suicide are to be explained by the fact that he had read North's translation rather than the original of Plutarch.

(337)

Wiley, Edwin, "A Study of the Supernatural in Three Plays of Shakespeare (1) *Julius Caesar,*" *U of California Chronicle,* 15 (1913): 490-501.

S's acceptance of certain Plutarchan elements in *JC* and his rejection of others is analyzed in the light of the supernatural effects which the playwright desired to achieve.

See also 30, 131, and 348.

THE INFLUENCE OF PLUTARCH ON *Timon*

(338)

Adams, J. Q. Jr., "The Timon Plays," *J of English and Germanic Philology*, 9 (1910) : 506-524. [S's sources, pp. 522-524.]

In writing *Timon*, S depended either upon North's Plutarch or upon Painter's *Palace of Pleasure*, but the evidence points to the former. He also depended, directly or indirectly, upon the manuscript play of Timon and upon material from Lucian's *Misanthropos*. Judging from S's use of every possible detail available in Plutarch's barren version, one must conclude that he obtained the outline of Lucian's story indirectly, since he omitted so many of its rich details.

(339)

Bertram, Franz, *Die Timonlegende: eine Entwicklungsgeschichte des Misanthropentypus in der antiken Literatur* [Greifswald], 1906, pp. 83-88 and *passim*.

In this analysis of the growth of the Timon legend, some space is devoted to the superiority of S's characterization of Timon as compared with his sources, Plutarch and Lucian, the latter of which was available to S in French and Italian translation.

(340)

Clemons, W. H., "The Sources of *Timon of Athens*," *Princeton U B*, 15 (1904) : 208-223.

A fairly detailed source discussion is followed by a table listing the probable points of indebtedness of *Timon* to North's Plutarch, Lucian, Painter, and the academic play on Timon. Although Boiardo is considered a possible source, his *Il Timone* is not included here among the probable sources.

(341)

Keller, Wolfgang, "*The Authorship of Timon of Athens* by Ernest Hunter Wright . . .". See 297.

From Plutarch S derived not only the name of Alcibiades' love, Timandra, but also, perhaps, *Timon,* III, v, 60-61 ("his service done At Lacedaemon and Byzantium . . .").

(342)

Wright, E. H., *The Authorship of Timon of Athens,* New York, 1910, pp. 8-23.

The sources of *Timon* are analyzed in an effort to throw light upon the authorship of the play. A tabulated list shows in how far S might have been influenced by Plutarch, Painter, Lucian, and the anonymous English comedy on the subject of Timon. S was not dependent upon Boiardo. See 297 and 341.

See also 335 and 452.

THE INFLUENCE OF PLUTARCH ON OTHER SN PLAYS

(343)

[Cowl, R. P.] *Sources of the Text of Henry the Fourth,* pp. 39-41. See 15.

A number of passages in Plutarch are cited as the sources of lines in *1* and *2H4*.

(344)

Johnstone, J.E., "The Classical Element in Shakespeare." See 16.

From Plutarch's letters in the original, S derived *AW*, IV, ii, 83 ("The web of our life is of mingled yarn, good and ill together").

(345)

Kittredge, G. L., "Shakespeare and Seneca?" *MLN*, 40 (1925) : 440.

M. L. Wilder (see 213) errs in suggesting Seneca as the source of two passages in *1H4*. Lady Percy's speech (*1H4*, II, iii, 42 ff.) was probably derived from Plutarch's "Life of Brutus" (1595 edition of North's translation, p. 1058) ; and the source of *1H4*, II, iii, 115-116 ("for I well believe Thou wilt not utter what thou dost not know") can be found in Nashe's *Anatomie of Absurdities* (McKerrow edition, I, 13-14).

(346)

Kröger, Ernst, *Die Sage von Macbeth bis zu Shakspere,* pp. 159, 228. See 39.

The reference to the moving stones (*Mac*, III, iv, 123) might have been derived from Plutarch or from Florio's translation of Montaigne. The allusion to Mark Antony's genius rebuked by Caesar (*Mac*, III, i, 56-57) was derived from Plutarch.

(347)

Sidgwick, Frank, *The Sources and Analogues of A Midsummer-Night's Dream (The Shakespeare Classics),* London, New York, 1908, pp. 9, 10, 12.

A number of minor details in *MND* are cited which were derived from Plutarch's "Life of Theseus."

(348)

Theobald, William, *The Classical Element in the Shakespeare Plays,* pp. 316-318. See 9.

Plutarch influenced not only *JC* and *AC* but also a passage in each of the following plays: *H, 2H4,* and *2H6.*

See also 166, 275, and 335.

Proclus

LATIN: Marsilius Ficinus, *Opera* [the excerpts from Proclus are in Vol. 2], Basel, 1576.

(349)

Rea, J. D., "Coleridge's Intimations of Immortality from Proclus," *MP,* 26 (1928) : 201-213. [S, p. 208.]
The same suggestion is made as in 350.

(350)

Rea, J. D., "Jaques on the Microcosm," *PQ,* 4 (1925) : 345-347.
Jaques' speech on the seven ages of man in *AYL* (II, vii, 140 ff.) was derived from the chapter beginning *"Aetates septem planetis septem congruae"* translated from Proclus by Ficinus in *Iamblichus de mysteriis Aegyptorum, Chaldaeorum, Assyriorum.*

Sophocles

LATIN AND GREEK-AND-LATIN: *Tragoediae omnes,* tr. J. B. Gabio, Venice, 1543.
Tragoediae quotquot extant septem, tr. I. Lalamantius, Paris, 1557.
Tragoediae VII, tr. Th. Naogeorgus, Basel [1558].
Tragoediae . . . quotquot extant, tr. G. Ratallerus, Antwerp, 1570.
Tragoediae VII, tr. Vitus Winsemius, Heidelberg, 1597.
Tragoediae selectae Aeschyli, Sophoclis, Euripidis [tr. Erasmus, Buchanan, et al., no pl.], 1567.
Ajax flagellifer, tr. I. Lonicerus, Basel, 1533.
Ajax lorarius, tr. J. Scaliger, Julii filii, Paris, 1573.

Antigone, tr. G. Hervetus in *Gentiani Herveti . . . quaedam opuscula,* Lyons, 1541.

Antigone, tr. T. Watson, London, 1581.

Philoctetes in Lemno, tr. Q. S. F. Christianus, Paris, 1586.

FRENCH: *Antigone,* tr. J. Ant. de Baïf, Paris, 1573.

Electra, tr. Lazare de Baïf, Paris, 1537.

ITALIAN: *Ajace flagellifero,* tr. Girolamo Giustiniano, Venice, 1603.

L'Antigone, tr. Luigi Alamanni [no pl.], 1533.

Edipo il Rè, tr. G. Giustiniano, Venice, 1589.

L'Edipo tiranno, tr. Orsatto Giustiniano, Venice, 1585.

Edipo tiranno, tr. M. P. Angelio Bargeo [Florence], 1589.

Eletra, tr. Erasmo di Valvasone, Venice, 1588.

SPANISH: *La vengança de Agamemnon* [*Electra*], tr. Fernan Perez de Oliva, Burgos, 1531.

GERMAN: *Ajax lorarius,* tr. M. W. S. M., Strassburg, 1608.

(351)

Johnstone, J. E., "The Classical Element in Shakespeare." See 16.

MV, IV, i, 377-378 ("you take my life When you do take the means whereby I live") was influenced by the passage in Sophocles' *Philoctetes* in which Achilles' son deprived a hunter of bow and arrow.

(352)

Robertson, J. M., *Did Shakespeare Write Titus Andronicus?* pp. 225-227. See 276.

The allusion to the burial of Ajax in *Titus,* I, i, 379-381, was derived from the *Ajax* of Sophocles. The fact that S was unable to read Greek and the fact that this Sophoclean work was not translated into English support the hypothesis that *Titus* was not written by S.

(353)

Sheppard, J. T., *Aeschylus and Sophocles,* p. 136. See 133.

S had probably read Latin and French versions of Sophocles. S was not acquainted with Aeschylus' writings despite apparent resemblances to them in some of his works.

(354)

Theobald, William, *The Classical Element in the Shakespeare Plays,* pp. 329-342. See 9.

Sophoclean dramas might have influenced passages in a number of Sn works. In some instances, however, there are also other possible sources of the Sn lines.

See also 93 and 310.

Tatius, see Achilles Tatius

Thucydides

ENGLISH: *The Hystory Writtone by Thucidides the Athenyan of the Warre Which Was betwene the Peloponesians and the Athenyans,* tr. Thomas Nicolls, London, 1550.

(355)

Jaggard, William, *Shakespeare Once a Printer and Bookman,* p. 27. See 2.

Although S's writings contain no reference to Thucydides by name, S probably read *The History of the Peloponnesian War.* Peloponnesus is mentioned in *AC,* III, viii, 40.

Xenophon

ENGLISH: *The Bookes of Xenophon Contayning the Discipline, Schole, and Education of Cyrus,* tr. [to the end of the sixth book only by] W. Barkar, London [1560?].

(356)

Jaggard, William, *Shakespeare Once a Printer and Bookman,* p. 28. See 2.

S's knowledge of Xenophon may be seen in *1H6,* II, iii, 5-6 ("I shall as famous be by this exploit As Scythian Tomyris by Cyrus' death").

CHAPTER THREE

Influence of French Literature on Shakespeare

Aubigné, Theodore Agrippa D'

(357)

Allen, Percy, *The Plays of Shakespeare and Chapman in Relation to French History*, London, 1933, pp. 21-50.

In order to support the thesis that S's plays were written by Lord Oxford and mirror Lord Oxford's political and religious experiences, passages are cited to show the influence of Aubigné's *Les Tragiques* on *Mac* and *KL*.

Bartas, see **Du Bartas**

Bellay, see 42 and 422.

Belleforest, François De and **Pierre Boisteau**

For bibliographical data, see **Bandello.**

INFLUENCE OF *Histoires tragiques* ON *H*

Couch, see Quiller-Couch.

(358)

Creizenach, W., "Hamletfragen," *SJ*, 42 (1906) : 76-85.

It is difficult to determine whether S's deviations from Belleforest are the result of modifications incorporated into the *Ur-H.*

(359)

Derocquigny, J., "Shakespeare et Belleforest," *Revue Anglo-Américaine,* 1 (1924) : 527-528.

S did not use the French version of Belleforest as the basis of *H* but depended upon the English translation, in an edition earlier than that of 1608.

(360)

Fagus, "Hamlet de Gascogne ou Shakespeare folk-loriste," *Minerve française*, 3 (1919) : 220-226.

Some Gascon tales resemble *H* more closely than Belleforest does. It is tentatively suggested that S might have obtained the tale by listening to some folk version of the story.

(361)

Gollancz, Sir Israel, *The Sources of Hamlet with Essay on the Legend*, London, 1926, xi, 321 pp.

Saxo Grammaticus, Belleforest, and *The Hystorie of Hamblet* are reprinted. There is an introductory essay on the Hamlet legend, but S's version is not discussed.

(362)

Marschall, Wilhelm, "Die Quellen der Polonius-Gestalt in *Hamlet*," *Germanisch-Romanische Monatsschrift*, 16 (1928) : 86-89.

Polonius combines characteristics of "le conseillier" found in Belleforest's version of Hamlet together with traits of the contemporary Danish "Staatskanzler" Romelius.

(363)

Morsbach, Lorenz, *Der Weg zu Shakespeare und das Hamletdrama: Eine Umkehr*, Halle a. S., 1922, pp. 49-71.

Although Kyd's *Ur-H* was undoubtedly the main source of *H*, S also used the French version of Belleforest. Conjectures are made regarding S's indebtedness to each of these sources.

(364)

Quiller-Couch, Sir A. T., *Shakespeare's Workmanship*, Cambridge, 1931, pp. 162-164.

Hamlet's harsh treatment of Ophelia is to be explained by the fact that she was a courtesan in the Belleforest version. S made her innocent but retained some vestiges of the older interpretation.

(365)

Trémolières, le Docteur, "Le Part de Belleforest (de Samatan) dans trois œuvres de Shakespeare," *Bulletin de la société archéologique*, *historique, littéraire et scientifique du Gers*, 39 (1938): 154-161, 201-207.

The Belleforest versions of *TN* and *MA* are summarized and compared with S's plays. Belleforest in the original French also might have influenced *H*, although it is possible that some English translation of Belleforest existed which has since been lost.

(366)

Walley, H. R., "Shakespeare's Conception of *Hamlet*," *PMLA*, 48 (1933): 777-798.

Although S probably obtained the material for *H* from an earlier English play on the subject, Belleforest's version is analyzed in an attempt to reconstruct this *Ur-H*.

(367)

Wiley, Edwin,"A Study of the Supernatural in Three Plays of Shakespeare," pp. 502-522. See 337.

Most of the supernatural paraphernalia in *H* was not derived from its source, Belleforest, but was original with S.

INFLUENCE OF *Histoires tragiques* ON SN WORKS OTHER THAN *H*

(368)

Hauvette, Henri, "Une variante française de la légende de Roméo et Juliette," *RLC*, 1 (1921): 329-337.

In the version of Boisteau (which is based upon that of Sevin) as in S's *RJ*, Romeo obtains poison from an apothecary, a character who does not occur either in Luigi da Porto or in Bandello. See 369.

(369)

Moore, O. H., "Le Rôle de Boaistuau dans le développement de la légende de Roméo et Juliette," *RLC*, 9 (1929): 637-643. [S, p. 638.]

Henri Hauvette's suggestion that S obtained the idea of the apothecary in *RJ* from Boisteau is probably correct. See 368.

(370)

Page, Nadine, "The Public Repudiation of Hero," *PMLA*, 50 (1935): 739-744.

Because the Elizabethan attitude toward women required the public denunciation and the public repudiation of Hero, S's *MA* deviated from Belleforest and Bandello.

See 427, 432, 434, and 464.

Boisteau, see Belleforest and 156 and 452.

Busche, Alexandre Van Den called Le Sylvain

ENGLISH: *The Orator: Handling a Hundred Severall Discourses in Forme of Declamations; Some of the Arguments Being Drawne from T. Livius and Other Auncient Writers, the Rest of the Authors Owne Invention,* tr. L[azarus] P[iot, i.e. Anthony Munday], London, 1596.

Several lists of *MV* sources mention Sylvain's *Orator* in passing.

(371)

Eberstadt, Rudolph, "Der Shylockvertrag und sein Urbild," *SJ*, 44 (1908): 1-35. [Especially pp. 24-25.]

From *The Orator* S could have obtained, almost verbatim, passages found in the trial scene of *MV* (IV, i).

See also 473.

D'Aubigné, see Aubigné

Du Bartas, Guillaume De Salluste

ENGLISH: *His Maiesties Poetical Exercises at Vacant Houres* [*The Furies* and *Lepanto,* tr. James I, King of Great Britain and Ireland], Edinburgh, 1591.
Babilon, a Part of the Seconde Weeke, tr. W. L'Isle, London, 1596.
The Colonies of Bartas, tr. W. Lisle [no pl.], 1598.
The Second Day of the Firste Weeke, tr. Tho. Winter, London, 1603.
The Third Dayes Creation, tr. T. Winter, London, 1604.
The Historie of Judith, tr. T. Hudson, Edinburgh, 1584.
Translations by J. Sylvester:
    The Triumph of Faith, London, 1594.
    The Sacrifice of Isaac; the Shipwracke of Jonas [London, 1592?].

The First Day of the Worldes Creation, London, 1595.

The Seconde Weeke, or Childhood of the World, London, 1598.

The Miracle of the Peace in France, Celebrated by the Ghost of Divine Du Bartas, London, 1599.

Bartas His Devine Weekes and Works [fragments and other small works of Bartas with other translations], London, 1605-1606.

Posthumous Bartas: The Third Day of His Second Week, London, 1607.

Posthumous Bartas: The Forenoon of the Fourth Day of His Second Week, London, 1607.

(372)

Dodge, R. E. N., "A Sermon on Source-Hunting," *MP,* 9 (1911) : 211-223. [S, pp. 212-214, 222-223.]

Sidney Lee errs in suggesting that Du Bartas influenced *VA.* [See 374.] The same characteristics of the horse mentioned in *VA* and Du Bartas' *Divine Weekes* are also to be found in Pulci's *Morgante maggiore.* The parallelism is the result of coincidence, not of borrowing. Sidney Lee's explanation of the relationship between *TN,* II, iii, 23 ff. ("In sooth, thou wast in very gracious fooling . . .") and Rabelais is also far-fetched. See 419.

(373)

Holmes, U. T., *The Works of Guillaume de Salluste, Sieur Du Bartas,* Chapel Hill, 1935, I: 157 n.

"All the world's a stage . . ." (*AYL,* II, vii, 139 ff.) should be compared with *Première sepmaine,* I, 147-151 *("Le monde est un theâtre . . .").*

(374)

Lee, Sidney, *The French Renaissance in England: An Account of the Literary Relations of England and France in the Sixteenth Century,* New York, 1910, p. 337 n.

The influence of Du Bartas, probably in the French version, may be seen in the description of the horse in *VA,* 271-274, 295-298, and 301-304. See 372.

(375)

Taylor, G. C., "Is Shakespeare's Antonio the 'Weeping Philosopher' Heraclitus?" *MP,* 26 (1928) : 161-167.

The similarity between the comparison of Antonio and Gratiano in *MV,*

I, i, and that of Heraclitus and Democritus cannot be dismissed as coincidence, nor is the essay on Heraclitus in Florio's Montaigne sufficiently close to be called S's source. S's source probably was the "Dialogue" in Sylvester's edition of *The Devine Weekes* which might have been available to S before its publication in 1605-1606.

Du Bellay, see 42 and 422.

Estienne, see 464.

Fevre, see **Le Fevre**

Froissart, Jean

ENGLISH: "Here begynneth the first, second, thirde, and fourthe boke of sir John Froissart of the cronycles of Englande, Fraunce, Spayne . . . ," tr. Johan Bourchier, knyghte lorde Berners, London, 1523-1525.

(376)

Anders, H., "Shakespeare und Froissart," *SJ,* 44 (1908) : 151.

1H6, I, ii, 29 ("Froissart, a countryman of ours . . .") was derived from Froissart in the original. It could not have been derived from Berner's translation nor from Holinshed, Grafton, nor Fabyan.

Garnier, Robert

ENGLISH: . . . *Antonius,* tr. Mary Herbert, Countess of Pembroke, London, 1592.

Cornelia, tr. T. Kidd, London, 1594.

(377)

Review: Boas, F. S., *"Shakespeare's Roman Plays and Their Background* by M. W. MacCallum," *MLR,* 7 (1912) : 110-113.

M. W. MacCallum does not do sufficient justice to the influence upon S of Kyd's translation of *Cornelia.* See 378.

(378)

MacCallum, M. W., *Shakespeare's Roman Plays*, pp. 628-630. See 253.

Although the verbal parallels between Garnier's *Cornélie*, in the French and English versions, and S's *JC* are not very close, there is a similarity of tone in the corresponding scenes. Parallel passages are quoted. See 377.

"Huon De Bordeaux"

ENGLISH: "Here begynneth the Boke of Duke Huon of Burdeuxe," tr. Sir John Bourchier, lord Berners, London [c. 1534-1540].

Several editions of *MND* and commentaries on that play mention *Huon of Bordeaux* as the ultimate or direct source of the name Oberon in S's comedy. Among the brief references to *Huon of Bordeaux* as a direct Sn source are the following:

(379)

Latham, M. W., *The Elizabethan Fairies: The Fairies of Folklore and the Fairies of Shakespeare (Columbia U Studies in English and Comparative Literature)*, New York, 1930, pp. 180-181.

(380)

Lee, Sidney, *The French Renaissance in England*, p. 96. See 374.

Larivey, see **Pasqualigo** and **Straparola**

Le Fevre, Raoul

ENGLISH: *The Recuile of the Histories of Troie*, tr. Wyllyam Caxton, London, 1553.

(381)

Stein, Elizabeth, "Caxton's *Recuyell* and Shakespeare's *Troilus*," *MLN*, 45 (1930): 144-146.

In *TC* S depended upon Caxton and was not directly influenced by Lydgate.

See also 281, 282, 283, 284, 290; also **Colonne, Guido Delle** and **Dictys.**

Lorris, Guillaume De

ENGLISH: *The Workes* of Geoffrey Chaucer, London [c. 1545]. [This edition contains the medieval English translation of selections from *Roman de la rose.*]

(382)

Ord, Hubert, *Chaucer and the Rival Poet in Shakespeare's Sonnets: A New Theory,* London and Toronto, 1921, 64 pp.

Chaucer was the Rival Poet referred to in S's *Sonnets.* These sonnets resemble *Roman de la rose* in philosophy, incidents, and wording.

(383)

Ord, Hubert, "A Source of the Sonnets: A New Interpretation," *London Shown by Shakespeare and Other Shakespearean Studies Including a New Interpretation of the Sonnets,* London, 1916, pp. 37-57.

The similarities between S's *Sonnets* and *Roman de la rose* are considered in detail.

Meung, Jean De, see Lorris, Guillaume De

Montaigne, Michel De

ENGLISH: *The Essayes,* tr. J. Florio, London, 1603.

(384)

Allen, Percy, "Montaigne and *Twelfth Night,*" *TLS,* September 18, 1937, p. 675.

In the forged letter to Malvolio (*TN,* II, v), "Moai" was intended as a cipher for Montaigne. In this letter, the advice given regarding Malvolio's conduct was derived from *Essais,* III, iii, and III, vii. The name Malvolio came from Montaigne's essay, "Des noms," where the words *"mal volontiers"* are to be found.

(385)

Bond, R. W., "Lucian and Boiardo in *Timon of Athens, MLR,* 26 (1931): 52-68.

From Florio's Montaigne, S obtained Holofernes' *"Venetia, Venetia . . ."* (*LLL,* IV, ii, 100).

(386)

Review: Bond, R. W., *"Montaigne and Shakespeare* by John M. Robertson," *MLR,* 5 (1910) : 361-370.

Although J. M. Robertson's main thesis is correct, he minimizes the influence of Montaigne on S before 1603 and exaggerates Montaigne's influence on the later plays. J. M. Robertson performs a service in showing that S could have obtained from Montaigne many passages which critics have suggested he derived from the classics, but he does not take sufficient account of the difference in the spirit of the two writers. See 28 n.

(387)

Chambrun, Mme. (Longworth), "Influences françaises dans la *Tempête* de Shakespeare," *RLC,* 5 (1925) : 37-59.

Passim references allude to the influence of Florio's Montaigne on *Tem.*

(388)

Collins, J. C., "Shakespeare and Montaigne," *Studies in Shakespeare,* Westminster, 1904, pp. 277-296.

Although S probably read Montaigne and did echo Montaignian sentiments in several passages in his plays, many of the alleged examples of S's dependence upon Montaigne are examples of coincidence rather than of borrowing.

(389)

Deutschbein, Max, "Shakespeares Kritik an Montaigne in *As You Like It,"* *Neuphilologische Monatsschrift,* 5 (1934) : 369-385.

Close parallels testify to S's borrowings from Montaigne in *AYL.* In fact, the character of Jaques might almost be called a personification of Montaigne. S could have seen a manuscript of the Florio translation before he wrote *AYL.*

(390)

Doran, Madeleine, "Elements in the Composition of *King Lear,"* SP, 30 (1933) : 34-58.

Attempting to show that textual irregularities in the *KL* quarto are indicative of Sn revision, the writer has made conjectures as to S's use of additional sources to enrich the later version. Although all the accepted *KL* sources are mentioned and the old *King Leir* play is considered in particular, great stress is placed upon S's use of various episodes in Sidney's *Arcadia* and of several essays of Montaigne.

(391)

Dowden, Edward, *Michel de Montaigne,* Philadelphia, London, 1905, p. 243.

H, II, ii, 323 ff. ("What a piece of work is a man . . .") might have been suggested by a passage from Montaigne's *Apologie of Raymond Sebond.*

(392)

Doyons, René-Louis, "Montaigne et Shakespeare," *Mercure de France,* 243 (1933): 246.

Although S could have obtained the concept from Plautus, Montaigne is the more probable source of *KL,* IV, i, 36 ff. ("As flies to wanton boys . . ."). See 400.

(393)

Review: Franz, W., "Shakespeare und Montaigne," *Die neueren Sprachen,* 40 (1932): 106-108.

The philosophy of both Montaigne and S was inspired by the classical and the Renaissance tradition. S's apparent indebtedness to Montaigne in *H* may be due to the fact that both writers had the same intellectual milieu. The explanation seems especially likely when one considers the difference in temperament between these two authors. See 409.

(394)

Gilbert, A. H., "Montaigne and *The Tempest,*" *Romanic R,* 5 (1914): 357-363.

Those resemblances between Montaigne's "Of Cannibals" and *Tem* which earlier critics have considered are cited, and some additional parallels are suggested.

(395)

Greenwood, G. G., *Is There a Shakespeare Problem?* pp. 125-127. See 64.

Despite J. M. Robertson's suggestion in *Montaigne and Shakespeare* [see 28 n.], MM, III, i, 116 ff. ("Ay, but to die and go we know not where . . .") was not derived from Montaigne's *Apologie of Raymond Sebond.*

(396)

Henderson, W. B. D., "Montaigne's *Apologie of Raymond Sebond* and *King Lear,*" *SAB,* 14 (1939): 209-225.

In *KL* S combined the plot of the old *King Leir* play with the philosophy expressed in Montaigne's *Apologie of Raymond Sebond.*

(397)

Review: Kellner, L., "Shakespeare und Montaigne," *Deutsche Rundschau,*
143 (1910): 140-153.

S read Montaigne in the Florio translation. The *Essais* did not lead the
playwright into new channels but strengthened already existing Sn characteristics. A careful analysis of so-called Montaignian influence suggests that
many of the parallels noted in Robertson's *Montaigne and Shakespeare* [see
28 n.] are far-fetched.

(398)

Lee, Sidney, *The French Renaissance in England,* pp. 168, 175-178. See
374.

Caution is necessary in estimating S's debt to Montaigne since many of
the similarities are in the realm of generally accepted Renaissance concepts.
Some of the more probable examples of S's dependence upon Montaigne are
analyzed.

(399)

M., L., "Montaigne et Shakespeare," *Mercure de France,* 242 (1933):
758-760.

Although Montaigne influenced the speech of Gonzalo in *Tem,* II, i,
154 ff. ("I' the commonwealth . . ."), many parallels which have been suggested between Montaigne and *MM, O, JC,* and *H* are the result of scholars'
ingenuity rather than of actual borrowing. It must, however, be admitted that
there is greater evidence of Montaignian influence after the publication of
the Florio translation than before it.

(400)

M., L., "Montaigne et Shakespeare," *Mercure de France,* 243 (1933):
506-507.

R. L. Doyons chooses to discuss one of the most questionable Sn parallels
to Montaigne which exists, one which could as easily have been derived
from Plautus as from Montaigne. See 392.

(401)

Magnus, Laurie, *English Literature in Its Foreign Relations,* London, 1927,
pp. 74-81.

The influence of Montaigne on *Tem* is considered in some detail.

(402)

May, Marcel, "Une influence possible de Montaigne sur Shakespeare dans *Henry V*, Acte IV, Scène 1," *Revue Anglo-Américaine*, 9 (1931): 109-126.

When writing *H5*, IV, i, S was influenced by a manuscript copy of Florio's translation of Montaigne. Parallels are cited to support this contention.

(403)

Norton, Grace, *The Spirit of Montaigne: Some Thoughts and Expressions Similar to Those in His Essays*, Boston, New York, 1908, pp. 49-72.

Passages from about half of S's works, including a number written before the publication of Florio's translation, are cited as evidence of S's dependence upon Montaigne.

(404)

Rea, J. D., "A Note on *The Tempest*," *MLN*, 35 (1920): 313-315.

To the generally accepted parallels between *Tem* and Montaigne's "Of Cannibals" should be added the fact that these two works are in agreement regarding the location and description of the island.

(405)

Robertson, J. M., *The Baconian Heresy*, p. 207 and *passim*. See 18.

H, V, i, 260 ff. ("Lay her i' the earth . . .") was not derived from Persius but from Montaigne's "Of Glory." Montaigne's *Essais* as well as other contemporary continental and English works are cited *passim* to illustrate the prevalence of certain Sn concepts.

(406)

Taylor, G. C., *Shakspere's Debt to Montaigne*, Cambridge, 1925, 66 pp.

Many passages are quoted to prove that S was greatly influenced by Montaigne and that this influence was strongest immediately after the publication of Florio's translation of the *Essais*. See 408.

(407)

Theobald, William, *The Classical Element in the Shakespeare Plays*, pp. 395-396. See 9.

Montaigne was not only the source of *Tem*, II, i, 154 ff. ("I' the commonwealth . . ."), but also was a possible source of *AYL*, II, i, 21 ff. ("Come, shall we go and kill us venison? . . .") and of *LLL,* IV, i, 24 ff. ("But come, the bow . . .").

(408)

Review: Tupper, J. W., *"Shakspere's Debt to Montaigne,"* *MLN,* 41 (1926) : 209-210.

G. C. Taylor's examples of S's indebtedness to Montaigne when taken individually may seem insignificant, but the vast array of parallels is impressive. These similarities might have been the result of subconscious recollection of pertinent passages in the *Essais* rather than the result of deliberate borrowing. See 406.

(409)

Türck, Susanne, *Shakespeare und Montaigne: Ein Beitrag zur Hamlet-Frage,* Berlin, 1930, 160 pp.

Not until he wrote *H* was S influenced by Montaigne. This influence, exerted through the Florio translation, was of greater significance in the field of ideas than in the field of actual verbal borrowings. A detailed list of parallels is offered. See 393.

(410)

Upham, A. H., *The French Influence in English Literature from the Accession of Elizabeth to the Restoration,* New York, 1908, pp. 280-286.

Some of the more significant parallels between Montaigne and S are cited.

(411)

Villey, Pierre, "Montaigne et les poètes dramatiques anglais du temps de Shakespeare," *Revue d'histoire littéraire de la France,* 24 (1917): 357-393. [S, pp. 381-393.]

Parallels between Montaigne and a number of Sn passages are analyzed but are discarded as insignificant.

(412)

Villey, Pierre, "Montaigne et Shakespeare" in *A Book of Homage to Shakespeare,* Oxford, 1916, pp. 417-420.

The towering edifice of parallelism between S and Montaigne is built on sand. The similarities in thought are merely coincidences, except for two or three passages in *H* whose indebtedness to Montaigne is questionable.

(413)

Wihan, Josef, *Die Hamlet-Frage: ein Beitrag zur Geschichte der Renaissance in England,* Leipzig, 1921, pp. 69-74.

The philosophy in *H* and in Florio's Montaigne are compared. The conclusion is drawn that although Montaigne had an enriching influence upon S, his *Essais* did not bring new philosophic concepts to S's attention.

See also 208, 229, 346, 375, 509, 568, 569, 571.

Paradin, Claude

ENGLISH: *The Heroicall Devises,* tr. P. T. London, 1591.

(414)

Fairchild, A. H. R., "A Note on *Macbeth.*" See 3.

Mac, I, v, 66-67 ("look like the innocent flower . . .") might have been suggested by Paradin's *Devises heroïques,* which was translated into English, or by Whitney's book of emblems.

Rabelais, François

GERMAN: *Affentheurlich naupengeheurliche Geschichtklitterung von . . . Grandgoschier, Gargellantua und . . . Pantagruel* [tr. J. Fischart], Gänsserich, 1552. [Only the first book is based on Rabelais.]

ENGLISH: Several references in the *Stationers' Register* suggest the possibility of a lost English translation.

(415)

Boulenger, Jacques, *Rabelais à travers les âges,* Paris, 1925, pp. 20-21.

Because the story of Gargantua and Pantagruel existed in Elizabethan oral tradition, it is difficult to determine whether S's allusions to it signify that he had read Rabelais' works, although this is probably the case.

(416)

Bourgeois, A.-F., "Rabelais en Angleterre," *Revue des études rabelaisiennes,* 3 (1905): 80-83.

Passages in Rabelais are cited as the source of lines in *KL, CE, LLL,* and *1H4.*

(417)

Brown, Huntington, *Rabelais in English Literature,* Cambridge, Mass., 1933, pp. 210-215 and *passim.*

Passages in over a dozen Sn plays are listed which might have been derived from Rabelais. It is noted, however, that *Mac,* II, iii, 5-6 ("a farmer that hanged himself on the expectation of plenty") was probably derived not from Rabelais but from Ben Jonson's *Every Man out of His Humour.*

(418)

Chambrun, Mme. (Longworth), "Influences françaises dans la *Tempête* de Shakespeare." See 387.

Passages from *Tem* are cited which might have depended upon Rabelais. Echoes of Rabelais are also noted in half a dozen other Sn plays.

(419)

Lee, Sidney, *The French Renaissance in England,* pp. 162-163. See 374.

The references to Gargantua (*AYL,* III, ii, 239 ff.), to Nero (*KL,* III, vi, 8-9), and to Pigrogromitus (*TN,* II, iii, 23 ff.), and the characterization of Holofernes in *LLL* show the influence of Rabelais. See 372.

(420)

Upham, A. H., *The French Influence in English Literature,* pp. 223, 237-242. See 410.

Rabelais might have been the source of passages in over a half dozen Sn plays, but the parallels cannot be pressed.

Ronsard, Pierre De

Because of the widespread influence of the Pleiade, no specific translations are cited here.

(421)

Bush, Douglas, *Mythology and the Renaissance Tradition in English Poetry,* p. 140. See 43.

Sidney Lee exaggerates the dependence of S's poems on the poems of the French Renaissance. Although certain lines of Ronsard could have been the source of part of *VA,* these lines are also to be found in Thomas Watson's eighty-third sonnet (*Poems,* Arber edition, p. 119).

(422)

Klein, David, "Foreign Influence on Shakespeare's Sonnets," *Sewanee R,* 13 (1905): 454-474.

The sixth sonnet of *Astrée* probably influenced S's twenty-fourth and one hundred and forty-fourth sonnets. Additional similarities exist between S and the French school of Ronsard and Du Bellay. Because of the widespread nature of Petrarchism, however, it is almost impossible to ascertain the direct sources of S's sonnet cycle.

(423)

Lee, Sidney, *The French Renaissance in England*, pp. 221-230, 266-276, and *passim*. See 374.

Passages from *VA* and from a number of other Sn works are cited to show the influence of Ronsard and the Pleiadic school on S.

"Roman De La Rose," see **Lorris, Guillaume De**

Salluste, see **Du Bartas**

Le Sylvain, see **Busche, Alexandre Van Den**

French Farces

(424)

Radoff, M. L., "Influence of The French Farce in *Henry V* and *The Merry Wives*," *MLN*, 48 (1933): 427-435.

The foreign language lessons in *MW* and *H5* might have been derived from similar lessons which are to be found in French farces.

CHAPTER FOUR

Influence of Italian Literature on Shakespeare

Alberti, Leon Battista

(425)

Clark, Kenneth, "Alberti and Shakespeare," *TLS*, March 26, 1931, p. 252.

The similarity between *H*, II, ii, 323 ff. ("What a piece of work is a man . . .") and Alberti's *Della tranquilità dell' animo* (*op. volg.* I, 70) might have been coincidental, but the parallelism is sufficiently marked to suggest that S might have read the Italian work in manuscript. It did not appear in print until 1843.

Aretino, Pietro

(426)

Lothian, J. M., "Shakespeare's Knowledge of Aretino's Plays," *MLR*, 25 (1930): 415-424.

Detailed parallels are cited to prove that over a dozen Sn works were influenced by Aretino's plays. S's impression that Julio Romano was a sculptor (*WT*, V, ii, 109) might have been the result of a quick skimming of Aretino's *Marescalco*, V, iii.

Ariosto, Lodovico

ENGLISH: "The Supposes," tr. George Gascoigne, printed in his *A Hundreth Sundrie Flowres*, London [1572]; in *The Posies of George Gascoigne*, London [1575]; in *The Whole Woorkes of George Gascoigne*, London, 1587.

Orlando Furioso in English Heroical Verse, tr. John Harington, London, 1591.

There are many brief references to the influence of *The Supposes* upon *TS*.

(427)

Bennet, M. L., "Shakespeare's *Much Ado* and Its Possible Italian Sources," *Studies in English,* No. 17 (*U of Texas B,* No. 3726), 1937, pp. 52-74.

A more probable source of *MA* than Bandello, either in the original or in the Belleforest translation, is to be found in Harington's translation of Ariosto's *Orlando furioso,* V. From this translation S probably derived most of the Hero-Claudio plot, Don John's villainy, the low-comedy subplot, and suggestions which he utilized in the creation of Beatrice and Benedick.

(428)

Charlton, H. B., *"The Taming of the Shrew,"* B of the John Rylands L, 16 (1932): 353-375.

The similarities and differences between classical, Italian, and English dramas are analyzed to explain S's use, in *TS,* of Ariosto's *Suppositi,* either in the Italian version or in the English version of Gascoigne.

(429)

Robertson, J. M., *The Baconian Heresy,* pp. 249-250. See 18.

The suggestion that "the prophetic fury" of *O,* III, iv, 73, was derived from the Italian of Ariosto's *Orlando furioso,* XLVI, 80, is unfounded. See 430.

(430)

Theobald, William, *The Classical Element in the Shakespeare Plays,* p. 388. See 9.

Brandes is quoted to the effect that *O,* III, iv, 71 ff. ("A sibyl . . .") was derived from *Orlando furioso* in the original, inasmuch as the phrase "prophetic fury" occurs in both *O* and the Italian of Ariosto but not in the Harington translation. See 429.

See also 434, 436, 498, and 561.

Bandello, Matteo

FRENCH: *Histoires tragiques extraictes des œuvres italiennes de Bandel,* tr. Pierre Boaistuau and François de Belleforest, Paris, 1559. [A number of supplements were published during the century.]

SPANISH: *Historias tragicas exemplares* [tr. Juan de Olave], Madrid, 1596.

Historias tragicas exemplares [tr. Vicente de Millis Godinez], Salamanca, 1589.

ENGLISH: *Certaine Tragicall Discourses,* tr. Geffraie Fenton [London, 1567].

The Hystorie of Hamblet [tr. from Belleforest], London, 1608.

["The most notable historie of John Lord Mandosse freely translated from the Spanish with additions by Thomas la Peend from the sixth tale in the French version of Bandello," no pl.], 1565.

William Painter, *The Palace of Pleasure,* London, 1566. [A number of Painter's tales are translated directly from Bandello or from the Belleforest-Boisteau translation.]

Note: Commentary on S's use of Brooke's *Romeus and Juliet* (in *RJ, TGV,* and *Sonnets*) is not included here. Although the title page of Brooke's work states that his work was "written first in Italian by Bandell," Brooke's poem does not follow the Italian version very closely.

See also 432 n.

(431)

Bush, Douglas, *Mythology and the Renaissance Tradition in English Poetry,* p. 150 n. See 43.

Bandello was not a source of *Lucrece.* Wilhelm Marschall's arguments that *Lucrece* was influenced by Bandello are weak. See 97.

(432)

Conrad, Hermann, "Zu den Quellen von Shaksperes *Twelfth Night," ESn,* 46 (1912): 73-85.

Of the possible sources of *TN, Riche His Farewell to the Militarie Profession* [see 464] is the most plausible. [Note: According to Morton Luce, Riche's book was probably based on Bandello and Belleforest, and it influenced both *TN* and *MND.*] Second in importance is Bandello. The *Gli inganni* plays seem to have had least bearing on *TN,* although they might have stimulated S's original interest in this type of plot.

(433)

Fitzmaurice-Kelly, James, *The Relations between Spanish and English Literature,* Liverpool, 1910, p. 20.

The similarities between Lope de Rueda's *Comedia de los engañados* and *TN* are to be explained by the fact that both these works were derived either from Bandello or from *Gli ingannati.*

(434)

Gaw, Allison, "Is Shakespeare's *Much Ado* a Revised Earlier Play?" *PMLA,* 50 (1935): 715-738.

The main source of the *MA* plot was Bandello's twentieth *novella,* either directly or indirectly, possibly through a now lost translation written by W. W. in 1580. It is improbable that S used the Belleforest version of Bandello, since *MA* does not contain the enrichments found therein. There is no foundation for the thesis that S used a lost English play on the subject of *MA,* nor should S's use of Ayrer's *Die schöne Phoenicia* be considered a possibility. Although Ariosto could not have served as the main source of *MA,* the window strategem was derived either from the English version of *Orlando furioso,* V, or from Spenser's *Faerie Queene,* II, iv.

(435)

Taylor, G. C., "Hermione's Statue Again (Shakspere's Return to Bandello)," *SAB,* 13 (1938): 82-86.

The twentieth tale of Bandello served as both the source of *MA* and of the second half of *WT.*

(436)

Wolff, M. J., "Zur Geschichte des Stoffes von *Much Ado About Nothing,*" *ESn,* 48 (1915): 342-348.

S's use of elements from da Porto, Ariosto, Bandello, *Die schöne Phoenicia,* and Giraldi in *MA* suggest his use of some unknown Italian drama which combined all these elements and, perhaps, of *Ariodante and Genevora,* an English dramatization of Ariosto's story.

See also **Belleforest** and 368, 370, 427, 464, 498, and 561.

Barberino, Andrea Da

(437)

Perott, Joseph de, "Shakespeare und die *Reali di Francia,*" *SJ,* 44 (1908): 153-154.

Over a dozen points of similarity are noted between Barberino's *Reali di Francia* and *Cym.* In some of the parallels noted, S might have used Lodovico Dolce's *Le prime imprese del Conte Orlando* instead of, or in addition to, the *Reali di Francia.*

Berni, Francesco

(438)

Fonblanque, E. M. de, "The Italian Sources of *Othello*," *The Fortnightly Review*, 96 (1911): 907-918.

Berni's *Orlando innamorato* and Guazzo's *La civile conversazione* in the Pettie translation both contain passages which are parallel to *O*, III, iii, 155 ("Good name in man and woman . . .").

(439)

Robertson, J. M., *The Baconian Heresy*, pp. 249-250. See 18.

"Who steals my purse . . ." (*O*, III, iii, 157) was not derived from Berni.

(440)

Theobald, William, *The Classical Element in the Shakespeare Plays*, p. 388. See 9.

O, III, iii, 157 ("Who steals my purse . . .") was derived from Berni's *Orlando innamorato*.

Boccaccio, Giovanni

FRENCH: *Des cent nouvelles*, tr. Laurens du Premierfait, Paris, 1485. *Le Decameron*, tr. Anthoine de Maçon, Paris, 1545.

SPANISH: *Cien novelas* [no tr.], Seville, 1496.

GERMAN: [*Decameron*] tr. Arigo [Heinrich Leubing?], Ulm [1473]. *Cento novella*, tr. Johannes Grüninger, Strassburg, 1519. *Kurtzweilige und lächerliche Geschichte und Historien* [revised and expanded by P. Johannes Pauli], Frankfort on Main, 1583.

DUTCH: *50 lustige Historien*, tr. Dirick Coornhert, Harlem, 1564.

ENGLISH: "Here begynneth the boke . . . the falle of princes . . . ," tr. John Lydgate, London, 1527. [This work was originally written in Latin.] William Painter, *The Palace of Pleasure*, London, 1566. [A number of Painter's tales were tr. from Boccaccio, including the version of "Helena of Florence" and "Giletta of Narbonne."]

(441)

Amos, F. R., *Shakespeare's Treatment of Sources in the Romantic Comedies*, MS Thesis, CL, 1909, pp. 20-25.

S's manipulation of "Giletta of Narbonne" is analyzed with special stress on the characterizations, dramatic structure, and plot additions of *AW*.

(442)

Bond, R. W., "The Puzzle of *Cymbeline,*" *Studia Otiosa,* London, 1938, pp. 69-74.

As a result of the attempted fusion of an Italian plot derived from one of Boccaccio's tales with an English historical background derived from Holinshed and Geoffrey of Monmouth, *Cym* contains anachronisms.

(443)

Hewlett, Maurice, "*All's Well That Ends Well,*" *19 C,* 91 (1922) : 964-971.

A comparison of *AW* with Boccaccio's version of the tale leads to the conclusion that the Italian *novella* is the more satisfactory.

(444)

Lawrence, W. W., "The Meaning of *All's Well That Ends Well,*" *PMLA,* 37 (1922) : 418-469.

S probably obtained Boccaccio's tale of "Giletta of Narbonne" from Painter's translation. It is summarized. *AW* is compared to it and to medieval analogues.

(445)

Lawrence, W. W., *Shakespeare's Problem Comedies, passim.* See 55.

It is difficult to determine whether S derived the plot of *Cym* directly or indirectly from Boccaccio. Painter's translation of Boccaccio was the source of *AW*. See 450.

(446)

Lawrence, W. W., "The Wager in *Cymbeline,*" *PMLA,* 35 (1920) : 391-431.

Although the exact source of *Cym* may never be known, the closest analogue to it is to be found in Boccaccio. *Cym* is compared to this and to other medieval and Renaissance versions of the tale.

(447)

Lee, A. C., "*Cymbeline:* The Source of the 'Wager Incident,' " *NQ,* Series 12, Vol. 1 (January-June 1916) : 342-343.

The wager incident in *Cym* was indebted not to *Westward for Smelts* but to Boccaccio's *Decameron*, either in the original or in some translation or adaptation.

(448)

Mechel, Kurt, *Die Historie von vier Kaufmännern (Le Cycle de la Gageure) und deren dramatische Bearbeitungen in der deutschen Literatur des XVI. und XVII. Jahrhunderts,* Halle a. S., 1914, pp. 60-62.

S's use of Boccaccio as the source of *Cym* is not as unquestionable as some critics maintain, since the first English translation of the *Decameron* did not appear until 1620. Although S's use of a French version of the *Decameron* is possible, *Frederick of Jennen,* an English folk book, contains all the points in which Boccaccio and S coincide.

(449)

Montgomery, Marshall, "Lydgate's *Fall of Princes* and *Hamlet*," *TLS*, October 16, 1924, p. 651.

The correspondent seeks corroboration of his theory that S derived the Gonzago story in *H* from Lydgate's translation of *De casibus*.

(450)

Review: "Shakespeare's Problem Plays," *TLS*, July 16, 1931, pp. 553-554.

In analyzing *AW* and *MM* one must neither neglect nor over-emphasize the importance of S's sources. On the one hand, S made the character of Bertram blacker than it had been in Boccaccio, and, on the other, he refined the crude characterizations of Giraldi and Whetstone into the humanized *dramatis personae* of *MM*. See 445.

(451)

Thrall, W. F., "*Cymbeline,* Boccaccio, and the Wager Story in England," *SP,* 28 (1931) : 639-651.

Although the *Decameron* is "the most satisfactory existing analogue" of *Cym* known, certain Sn elements, which are absent from the Boccaccian version, do occur in *Westward for Smelts, Frederick of Jennen,* and other analogues of the tale. This fact suggests S's dependence upon some unknown source.

See also 125 and 514.

Boiardo, Matteo Maria

(452)

Bond, R. W., "Lucian and Boiardo in *Timon of Athens."* See 385.

Detailed citations are offered to support the thesis that Boiardo's *Timone* influenced S's *Timon.* The echoes of Lucian, noted by some critics, came into the Sn play *via* Boiardo. Plutarch was of less importance as a source than Boiardo, and elements of the Sn play which have been credited to the influence of Painter might, more probably, have been derived from John Alday's translation of Boisteau's *Theatrum mundi.*

See also 340 and 342.

Castiglione, Baldassare

ENGLISH: *The Courtyer,* tr. Thomas Hoby, London, 1561.

(453)

Baughan, D. E., "Shakespeare's Probable Confusion of the Two Romanos," *J of English and Germanic Philology,* 36 (1937): 35-39.

In Hoby's translation of *The Courtier,* the sculptor Johnchristopher Romano is mentioned *(Tudor Translations,* 1900, pp. 93-94) two pages after the name, Julian, appears in capital letters. This fact may explain S's confusion in *WT,* V, ii, 109, of the painter Giulio Romano with the sculptor, Johnchristopher Romano.

(454)

Sullivan, Edward, "An Italian Book of Etiquette in Shakespeare's Day," *19 C,* 73 (1913): 1270-1285. [P. 1271.]

In his edition of *The Courtier* [1901], Sir Walter Raleigh suggested that S was dependent upon Castiglione, but his arguments are too weak to bear scrutiny.

(455)

Wales, J. G., "Shakespeare's Use of English and Foreign Elements in the Setting of *The Two Gentlemen of Verona," Transactions of the Wisconsin Academy of Sciences, Arts and Letters,* 27 (1932): 85-125. [P. 85.]

To support a statement that S was influenced by Castiglione when writing *MA,* reference is made to the following article by M. A. Scott: *"The Book* of the Courtier, a Possible Benedick and Beatrice," *PMLA*, 16 (1901): 475-502.

Cecchi, Giovammaria

(456)

Bond, R. W., "The Framework of *The Comedy of Errors*," pp. 43-50. See 226.

After a brief demonstration of the fact that Plautus had a greater influence upon S than Terence did, detailed support is offered for the thesis that Cecchi's *L'Ammalata* was the source of the framework of *CE*.

See also 240.

Cintio, see Giraldi

"Commedia Dell' Arte"

(457)

Campbell, O. J., "*Love's Labour's Lost* Re-studied" in *Studies in Shakespeare, Milton, and Donne* by Members of the English Department of the U of Michigan, New York, 1925, pp. 3-45. [*Commedia dell' arte*, pp. 23-44.]

Detailed parallels are noted between characters of the *commedia dell' arte* and the group of comics in *LLL*. See 462 and 467.

(458)

Campbell, O. J., "*The Two Gentlemen of Verona* and Italian Comedy" in *Studies in Shakespeare, Milton, and Donne*, pp. 47-63. See 457.

The close similarity between *TGV* and *commedie dell' arte* in plots, romantic dialogue, and characters suggests that S's source was a strongly Italianate play. It might have been the lost *Felix and Philiomena*, which superimposed Italianate qualities upon a plot derived from *Diana* of Montemayor. See 462, 467, and 548.

(459)

Chambers, E. K., "The Integrity of *The Tempest*," *RES*, 1 (1925): 129-150. [P. 133.]

H. D. Gray's suggestion that the *commedia dell' arte* influenced *Tem* depends too much upon hypothesis. There is no evidence that Italian *scenari* were performed in London. Visits to London by Italian actors, moreover, were rare at this period. See 461.

(460)

Coulter, C. C., "The Plautine Tradition in Shakespeare." See 143.

Classical dramatic conceptions which came to S through Italian comedy are noted *passim* as are S's allusions to the characters and dramatic conventions of the *commedia dell' arte.*

(461)

Gray, H. D., "The Sources of *The Tempest*," *MLN*, 35 (1920) : 321-330.

Eslava's *Noches de invierno,* Ayrer's *Die schöne Sidea,* and *The Mirrour of Princely Deeds and Knighthood* should be discarded as sources of *Tem* in favor of *commedie dell' arte,* a number of which show marked similarities to *Tem.* See 459, 528, and 531.

(462)

Henneberger, O. P., *Proximate Sources for the Italianate Elements in Shakespeare.* See 151.

With the possible exception of certain elements in *Tem,* S obtained from his grammar school studies of such writers as Plautus and Terence the material which O. J. Campbell [see 457 and 458] and K. M. Lea [see 463] credit to the influence of the *commedia dell' arte.* See 151 and 550.

(463)

Lea, K. M., *Italian Popular Comedy,* II: 431-454 and *passim.* See 153.

Similarities between the *commedia dell' arte* and *MW, CE,* and *Tem* are analyzed in detail. There are scattered references to the influence on S of stock characters and situations found in the *commedia dell' arte.* See also 153, 462, 468, and 497.

(464)

Luce, Morton, ed., *Rich's Apolonius and Silla: An Original of Shakespeare's Twelfth Night,* London, 1912, xii, 96 pp.

In writing *TN* S was probably influenced by *Gli ingannati,* several plays entitled *Gl' inganni,* a Bandello *novella* which is a version of the *Gli ingannati* tale, Belleforest's translation of the Bandello tale, and Rich's *Apolonius and Silla.* Selections from each of these sources are reprinted.

S might have received some suggestions from the Latin version of *Gli ingannati: Laelia.* Less stress should be placed on the possibility of S's having been acquainted with *Les Abusés* by Charles Estienne, or with Giraldi's Italian version or any of the Spanish versions of *Gli ingannati*. Minor details in *TN* were derived from Pliny, Saviolo's *Practice of the Duello*, Guazzo's *Civile Conversation*, and Erasmus' *Adagia*. See 432.

(465)

Vollhardt, W., "Zur Quellenkunde von Shakespeares *Sturm*," *Beiblatt zur Anglia*, 37 (1926) : 337-342.

Parallels to *Tem* in Italian eclogues, shepherd dramas, and *commedie dell' arte* are considered in detail. Special stress is laid on the possible influence of the *commedia dell' arte*.

(466)

Wolff, M. J., "Shakespeare und die *Commedia dell' arte*." See 161.

S probably saw performances of the *commedia dell' arte* in England. Over half a dozen Sn plays show the influence of the *commedia dell' arte*. Parallels are noted in detail. See 484.

(467)

Wright, L. B., "Will Kemp and the *Commedia dell' arte*," *MLN*, 41 (1926) : 516-520.

O. J. Campbell [see 457 and 458] is correct in crediting to the influence of the *commedia dell' arte* much of S's early comedy which previously has been attributed to the influence of Lyly. S took advantage of Will Kemp's familiarity with the *commedia dell' arte* when he wrote for Kemp the parts of Launce in *TGV* and of Costard in *LLL* as well as the characters of Peter in *RJ* and of Dogberry in *MA*.

(468)

Yates, F. A., *A Study of Love's Labour's Lost*, Cambridge, 1936, pp. 173-182.

Some of K. M. Lea's suggestions regarding the influence of the *commedia dell' arte* on *LLL* [see 463] are accepted, and additional material is supplied to strengthen the hypothesis.

See 432 and 433.

Dante Alighieri

Since the general trend of criticism is exemplified by the annotation below, a list of the translations of Dante is omitted.

(469)

Kuhns, [L.] Oscar, *Dante and the English Poets from Chaucer to Tennyson,* New York, 1904, pp. 70-79.

Although there are many alleged cases of Dante's influence on S, these parallels are inconclusive or questionable.

Dolce, Lodovico

(470)

Perott, Joseph de, "Über die Quelle von Shakespeares *Cymbeline,*" *Philologiae Novitates—Wissenschaftlichen Beiträgen,* 3 (1907) : 6-7.

The source of *Cym* was Lodovico Dolce's *Le prime imprese del Conte Orlando.* This Italian work is summarized and compared with the Sn play. It is uncertain whether S also obtained material for *Cym* from Antonio de Eslava's *Noches de invierno* in which the form "Sienna" rather than the un-Sn "Sutri" is used.

See also 437 and 499.

Doni, A. F., see 511.

Fiorentino, see **Giovanni**

Fortini, Pietro, see 511.

Giovanni, Fiorentino

There are a number of brief references to the effect that Giovanni's *Il pecorone,* IV, 1, was the direct or indirect source of *MV.*

(471)

Griston, H. J., *Shaking the Dust from Shakespeare: An Authentic Renovation of The Merchant of Venice,* New York, 1924, Sources: pp. 168-199.

Giovanni's *novella* is the closest known analogue to *MV.* S, however, might have made use of some intermediary play which has since been lost.

(472)

Rea, J. D., "Shylock and the Processus Belial," *PQ*, 8 (1929): 311-313.

In order to make *MV* attractive to his audience, S blended other elements with his main source which was a *novella* by Giovanni.

(473)

Scott, M. A., *Elizabethan Translations from the Italian*, Boston and New York, 1916, p. 59.

Il pecorone, IV, 1, resembles *MV* more closely than either the tale on the same subject in *Gesta Romanorum* or in *The Orator*.

See also 512.

Giraldi Cintio, Giovanni Battista

FRENCH: *Premier (et deuxième) volumes des cent excellent nouvelles* [tr. Gabriel Chappuys], Paris, 1583 or 1584. [This tr. contains versions of both *MM* and *O*.]

SPANISH: [*Hecatommithi*] tr. Luys Gaytan de Vozmediano, Toledo, 1590.

ENGLISH: *The Right Excellent and Famous Historye of Promos and Cassandra; Devided into Two Commicall Discourses* by George Whetstone, London, 1578.

An Heptameron of Civil Discourses by George Whetstone, London, 1582. [The second story of the Fourth Day's Exercise is tr. from *Hecatommithi*.]

(474)

Albrecht, Louis, *Neue Untersuchungen zu Shakespeares Mass für Mass: Quellen, Zeit und Anlass der Entstehung des Stückes und seine Bedeutung als Offenbarung der persönlichen Weltanschauung des Dichters*, Berlin, 1914, pp. 5-163.

Whetstone and Giraldi each wrote a drama and a tale which served S as the main sources of *MM*. *Basilikon Doron* by James I of England, also a significant source of *MM*, has been neglected by previous critics. See 478.

(475)

Budd, F. E., "Material for a Study of the Sources of Shakespeare's *Measure for Measure*," *RLC*, 11 (1931): 711-736.

A comparison of *MM* and its analogues leads to the conclusion that S was dependent upon Whetstone's *Promos and Cassandra,* and, perhaps, upon Giraldi's *novella,* Giraldi's *Epitia,* and *The Second Part and Knitting Up of the Boke Entituled Too Good to Be True* by Thomas Lupton.

(476)

Bullock, W. L., "The Sources of *Othello,*" *MLN,* 40 (1925) : 226-228.
A. H. Krappe's thesis (see 481) is refuted.

(477)

Chambers, R. W., "The Jacobean Shakespeare and *Measure for Measure,*" *Proceedings of the British Academy,* 1937, *passim.*

How S manipulated his *MM* sources (Whetstone's *Promos and Cassandra* and, perhaps, Whetstone's prose tale and Giraldi's *Epitia* and *novella*) in order to make his version milder and more palatable is considered in detail.

(478)

Review: Creizenach, *"Neue Untersuchungen zu Shakespeares Mass für Mass . . . von . . .* Louis Albrecht," *SJ,* 51 (1915) : 264-268.

Of the sources of *MM* suggested by Louis Albrecht [see 474], Whetstone's play has the strongest claim. The only important parallel to Whetstone's prose tale is the name Isabella. The suggested parallels between *MM* and *Epitia,* between *MM* and Giraldi's *novella,* and between *MM* and *Basilikon Doron* are weak.

(479)

Draper, J. W., "Desdemona: A Compound of Two Cultures," *RLC,* 13 (1933) : 337-351.

Those elements in the characterization of Desdemona which are not to be found in Giraldi are the result of welding together the Italian concept with the English attitude toward women.

(480)

Fonblanque, E. M. de, "The Italian Sources of *Othello.*" See 438.

This article, largely based upon an essay by Carlo Segrè, compares *O* with Giraldi's versions of the story.

(481)

Krappe, A. H., "A Byzantine Source of Shakespeare's *Othello,*" *MLN,* 39 (1924) : 156-161.

The discrepancies between the versions of S and Giraldi suggest that *O* was derived not from Giraldi but from another version of the Byzantine epic. See 476.

(482)

Lawrence, W. W., *Shakespeare's Problem Comedies,* pp. 84-94. See 55.

Although *MM* might have been indebted to Giraldi's *novella* and play for minor suggestions, only its indebtedness to Whetstone's play is of great significance.

(483)

Squire, J. C., *Life and Letters: Essays,* New York [c. 1921], pp. 152-158.

An analysis of Giraldi's *novella* and *O* suggests that the tragic ending of S's play is illogical.

(484)

Wokatsch, Werner, "Zur Quelle des *Othello* und zu Shakespeares Kenntnis des Italienischen," *Ar,* 162 (1932) : 118-119.

There were intermediaries between S and his Italian sources of *RJ, MV,* and *MM.* Gabriel Chappuys' French translation of Giraldi, which has recently been discovered, has been suggested as such an intermediary between *O* and the Italian of Giraldi. However, this translation lacks the line "Give me the ocular proof," which is to be found both in the original of Giraldi and in S's *O,* III, iii, 361, 365. This would suggest that S did obtain the story of *O* directly from the Italian of Giraldi. If that is the case, he might also have been influenced by plays of the *commedia dell' arte,* as M. J. Wolff has suggested. See 466.

See also 436, 450, 464, and 495.

Guazzo, Stefano

ENGLISH: *The Civile Conversation,* tr. from the French of Gabriel Chappuys by George Pettie, The Fourth Volume tr. from the Italian by B. Young, London, 1586.

(485)

Sullivan, Edward, "A Forgotten Volume in Shakespeare's Library," *19 C,* 55 (1904) : 267-277.

Examples are cited to show the influence of Guazzo on over a dozen Sn works.

(486)

Sullivan, Sir Edward, ed., M. S. Guazzo, *The Civile Conversation, the First Three Books Translated by George Pettie, Anno 1581 and the Fourth by Barth. Young, Anno 1586* (*The Tudor Translations*, Second Series, ed. Charles Whibley, Vol. VII), London, New York, 1925, pp. xxxviii-xcii.

Passages from over a score of Sn works show the influence of Guazzo.

(487)

Sullivan, Edward, "An Italian Book of Etiquette in Shakespeare's Day." See 454.

This article, a supplement to "A Forgotten Volume in Shakespeare's Library," adds to the number of Sn passages which might have been influenced by Guazzo.

See also 438 and 464.

Guicciardini, Lodovico

FRENCH: *Les Heures de recreation,* tr. F. de Belleforest, Paris, 1573.

GERMAN: *Erquickstunden. Von allerley kurtzweiligen Historien . . . ,* tr. D. Federman von Memmingen, Basel, 1574.

ENGLISH: *The Description of the Low Countreys and of the Provinces thereof Gathered into an Epitome* [by T. Danett], London, 1593.

(488)

Jaggard, William, *Shakespeare Once a Printer and Bookman,* p. 14. See 2.

In his *Description of the Low Countries,* Guicciardini described how letters were cut out of bark in early printing. This might have been the source of *AYL,* III, ii, and of Costard's name in *LLL.*

(489)

Krappe, A. H., "The Source of *Othello,* Act III, sc. iii, ll. 157-61," *MLR,* 23 (1928): 44-45.

Guicciardini's *Ore di recreazione* (in the series *Classici del ridere,* Rome, 1924, p. 36, no. 56) might have been the source, directly or indirectly, of *O,* III, iii, 157 ("Who steals my purse steals trash . . .").

Machiavelli, Niccolo

LATIN: . . . *De principe libellus,* tr. Sylvester Telius, Basel, 1560.

De Italiae statu antiquo et novo libri quatuor, adversus Machiavellum by T. Bozius, Cologne, 1594.

Florentini princeps . . . [tr. Sylvester Telius] *adjecta sunt ejusdem argumenti aliorum quorundam contra Machiavellum scripta* . . . [Basel?], 1589.

FRENCH: *Le Prince,* tr. Guillaume Cappel, Paris, 1553.

Le Prince, tr. Gaspard d'Auvergne, Poitiers, 1563.

Le Prince, tr. Jacques Gohory, Paris, 1571.

Discours sur les moyens de bien gouverner [*l'Antimachiavel*] by Innocent Gentillet [Geneva], 1576.

Decade de Tite Live, tr. Jacques Gohory, Paris, 1571.

. . . *Decade de Tite Live,* tr. Gaspard d'Auvergne, Paris, 1571.

Traité des conjurations extraict du troisième livre des discours [tr. J. Chomedey], Paris, 1575.

L'Histoire de Castrucci Castracani [tr. G. Guillet de Saint George], Paris, 1571.

La Vie de Castruccio Castracani, souverain de Lucques, tr. M. Dreux Du Radier, Paris, 1573.

ENGLISH: Innocent Gentillet, *A Discourse upon the Meanes of Wel Governing a Kingdome: Against N. Machiavel,* tr. S. Paterick, London, 1577.

Florentine Historie Written in the Italian Tongue, tr. T. B., London, 1595.

The Arte of Warre . . . *(Certain Waies of the Orderyng of Souldiers),* tr. P. Whitehorne, London, 1573.

(490)

Boyer, C. V., *The Villain as Hero in Elizabethan Tragedy, passim.* See 178.

There are scattered references to the Machiavellianism of such Sn characters as Aaron of *Titus* and Richard the Third.

(491)

Deutschbein, M., "Shakespeare und die Renaissance," *Die neueren Sprachen,* 23 (1916): 9-21. [P. 14.]

R3 is a synthesis of Marlowe, Machiavelli, and classical drama of Seneca. Richard represents the Marlovian type supporting the principles of Machiavelli's *Il principe.* The eighteenth chapter of *The Prince* may be considered a commentary on S's play.

(492)

Henneke, Agnes, "Shakespeares englische Könige im Lichte staatsrecht-licher Strömungen seiner Zeit," *SJ,* 66 (1930) : 79-144.

The influence of Gentillet's translation of Machiavelli on the Sn conception of statecraft and royalty is noted *passim.*

(493)

Lewis, Wyndham, *The Lion and the Fox: the Rôle of the Hero in the Plays of Shakespeare,* London, 1927, pp. 71 ff.

A table is given of Gentillet's version of Machiavelli's maxims, which S probably read.

(494)

Magnus, Laurie, *English Literature in Its Foreign Relations,* pp. 58-72. See 401.

S's modifications of Marlowe's Machiavellianism made for a broader out-look.

(495)

Praz, Mario, "Machiavelli and the Elizabethans," *Proceedings of the British Academy,* 14 (1928) : 49-98.

It is uncertain whether S had direct access to Machiavelli's writings. The character of Iago, which is Machiavellian, was derived from Giraldi. The character of Claudius in *H* shows no direct borrowings from Machiavelli.

Masuccio, Salernitano

Brief references to Masuccio as a source of *MV* occur in some editions of that play.

(496)

Griston, H. J., *Shaking the Dust from Shakespeare: An Authentic Reno-vation of The Merchant of Venice.* See 471.

The Jessica story of *MV* was probably derived from the fourteenth tale of Masuccio.

(497)

Lea, K. M., *Italian Popular Comedy,* II: 392. See 153.

Shylock's playing the part of the typical father of an Italianate love intrigue need not necessarily be attributed to the influence of the *commedia dell' arte*, but may be the result of the influence on *MV* of *The Jew of Malta* or a *novella* of Masuccio.

Oddi, Sforza Degli, see 241.

Pasqualigo, Luigi

FRENCH: *Le Fidelle*, tr. Pierre de Larivey in his *Trois nouvelles comédies*, Troyes and Paris, 1611.

ENGLISH: *The Pleasaunt and Fine Conceited Comoedie of Two Italian Gentlemen* by A. M. [no pl., c. 1580].

LATIN MANUSCRIPT: *Comoedia Latina per Abrahamum Fransum ad Philippum Sydneium* [1583]. Now known as *Victoria*.

Several bibliographies state categorically that 1611 is the earliest date of publication of Larivey's last three comedies, but F. C. Lonchamp *(Manuel du bibliophile français (1470-1920),* Paris and Lausanne, 1927, II:267) after citing a 1611 edition of *La Constance, Le Fidelle,* and *Les Tromperies* observes: *"Toutes trois avaient déjà été imprimées séparément."* Although Huntington Library, New York Public Library and the Library of Congress were so kind as to join in the search, we have been unable to find any edition of *Le Fidelle* prior to 1611.

(498)

Danchin, F. C., "Une Source de *Much Ado About Nothing,"* *Revue Anglo-Américaine,* 13 (1936) : 430-431.

Since the character of Don Pedro is absent from Bandello's version of the tale, attempts have been made to discover the original of *MA* in Ariosto's *Orlando Furioso* or Spenser's *Faerie Queene.* A closer parallel, however, exists in *A Pleasaunt Comoedie of Two Italian Gentlemen* by A. M.

(499)

Lee, Sidney, *The French Renaissance in England,* pp. 422-427. See 374.

S was influenced by the French *Le Fidelle,* as well as by Munday's English translation, when he wrote *TGV.* The comic elements of *LLL, MW,* and *TS* also show a marked similarity in tone to the badinage found in Larivey's *Le Fidelle,* adapted from Luigi Pasqualigo's *Il fedele,* and Larivey's *Le Laquais,* adapted from Lodovico Dolce's *Ragazzo.*

Pescetti, Orlando

(500)

Ayres, H. M., and H. M. MacCracken, "Shakespeare and Pescetti," *N*, 90 (1910) : 584-585.

Although there are some parallels between Shakespeare's *JC* and Pescetti's *Cesare,* these similarities are probably the result of coincidence rather than of borrowing.

(501)

Boecker, Alexander, *A Probable Italian Source of Shakespeare's Julius Caesar,* New York, 1913, viii, 130 pp.

JC was probably influenced by the *Cesare* of Pescetti, and much material that was formerly attributed to the influence of Appian was, actually, derived from Pescetti. See 251 and 504.

(502)

Cipriani, Lisi, "A Source of Shakespeare's *Julius Caesar,*" *N*, 90 (1910) : 556.

Verbal and stylistic similarities between *JC* and *Cesare* are listed.

(503)

Robertson, J. M., "The Origination of *Julius Caesar,*" *The Shakespeare Canon,* London, 1922, I: 150-151.

The echoes of Pescetti's *Cesare* which are to be found in *JC* were introduced by Chapman.

(504)

Review: Wolff, M. J., "Alexander Boecker, *A Probable Italian Source of Shakespeare's Julius Caesar,*" *ESn,* 48 (1915) : 441-443.

The parallels noted between Pescetti's and S's dramas on the subject of Caesar are largely ideological rather than verbal and are, therefore, inconclusive. See 501.

See also 332.

Petrarch, Francesco

Because of the widespread nature of the Petrarchan cult, few critics have attempted to prove the direct influence of Petrarch on S. Because a list of the formal translations of the Italian poet could not do justice to his influence during the Renaissance, a tabulation of translations is omitted here.

(505)

Borghesi, Peter, *Petrarch and His Influence on English Literature,* Bologna, 1906, pp. 106-113.

Although S was influenced by Petrarch and Petrarchists, he, himself, was not a member of the Petrarchan school.

(506)

Conrad, Hermann, "Petrarca als Lyriker verglichen mit seinem grössten Jünger, Shakspere," *Preussische Jahrbücher,* 166 (1916): 376-388.

Echoes of Petrarch are noted in the speeches of Romeo.

(507)

H., E., "A Note on Shakespeare and Petrarch," *Anglo-Italian R,* 5 (1919): 45-46.

S's Sonnet CX imitated not only the sentiment but also the wording of *In Vita di Madonna Laura.*

(508)

Hutton, Edward, "Shakespeare and Petrarch," *TLS,* May 12, 1921, p. 308.

This article makes the same contribution as 507.

(509)

Wolff, M. J., "Shakespeare und der Petrarkismus," *Die neueren Sprachen,* 28 (1920): 193-203.

This detailed article deals with the influence of Petrarchism on S's works, but the specific sources of S's Petrarchistic borrowings are not cited. *RJ* contains the last traces of Petrarchism to be found in S as well as the beginnings of a completely antithetical influence on S—that of Montaigne.

Porto, Luigi Da

(510)

Moore, O. H., "Shakespeare's Deviations from *Romeus and Juliet,*" *PMLA,* 52 (1937): 68-74.

In four instances in which S's important characters deviate from Brooke's poem, *RJ* agrees with the original version of Luigi da Porto of which no known English or French translation was in existence. Although one may either ignore this indebtedness to da Porto or assume a lost intermediary play, S had, probably, direct or indirect contact with Luigi da Porto's own version of the tale.

See also 368 and 436.

Straparola, Giovanni Francesco

FRENCH: *Les Facecieuses Nuits* [tr. J. Louveau and P. de Larivey], Paris, 1585.

ENGLISH: *Newes out of Purgatory* by Richard Tarlton [London? 1590?]. William Painter, *The Palace of Pleasure,* London, 1566, I, xlix.

Several editions of *MW* include Straparola in the original or in the Tarlton version as a possible source of *MW*.

(511)

Forsythe, R. S., "*The Merry Wives of Windsor:* Two New Analogues," *PQ,* 7 (1928) : 390-398.

MW combines Straparola's "The Two Lovers of Pisa" (as found in Tarlton's *Newes out of Purgatory*) and Straparola's "Philenio Sisterna" (in the Painter version) with Plautus' *Casina.* S was probably not acquainted with the following two analogues of *MW:* A. F. Doni's "The Bolognese Doctor and the Foolish Student" and Pietro Fortini's "The Florentine Doctor and the Student." See also 162.

(512)

Vollhardt, William, "Ein italienischer Falstaff," *Studien zur vergleichenden Literaturgeschichte,* 7 (1907) : 110-117.

Neither Giovanni's nor Straparola's *novella* is sufficiently close to have been the source of *MW*. A much closer analogue is an Italian comedy, *Atalanta,* 1610. Although this could not have been S's source, both *MW* and *Atalanta* might have been dependent upon a common source.

Tasso, Torquato

LATIN: *Amyntas* by T. Watson [London], 1585. [Note in *Short Title Catalogue* of Pollard and Redgrave: "The indebtedness of this Latin poem to Tasso has been greatly exaggerated and it should have been entered under Watson."]

ENGLISH: *The Lamentations of Amyntas,* tr. A. Fraunce in English hexameters from the Latin version of Watson in *The Countesse of Pembrokes Yvychurch, Conteining the Affectionate Life and Unfortunate Death of Phillis and Amyntas,* London, 1591.

Godfrey of Bulloigne or the Recoverie of Hierusalem, tr. R. C[arew], London, 1594.

Godfrey of Bulloigne, tr. E. Fairefax, London, 1600.

(513)

[Cowl, R. P.] *Sources of the Text of Henry the Fourth,* pp. 36-37. See 15.

Daniel's "A Pastorall," translated from a chorus in Tasso's *Amyntas,* I, ii, was the source of *1H4,* V, i, 136 ("What is honour? a word . . .").

(514)

Greenlaw, Edwin, "Shakespeare's Pastorals," *SP,* 13 (1916): 122-154. [Pp. 136-147.]

Detailed parallels are cited to show that *Cym* was derived from the story of Erminia in books seven and nineteen of Tasso combined with the wager theme found in Boccaccio, the star-crossed lover theme of *RJ,* and material from Holinshed.

(515)

Lee, Sidney, "Tasso and Shakespeare's England," *Elizabethan and Other Essays,* ed. F. S. Boas, Oxford, 1929, p. 176.

The name Sylvia for the character in *TGV* was taken from the name of the heroine of *Amyntas.* Tasso's influence may also be seen in *LLL,* IV, iii, 302, ("From women's eyes this doctrine I derive . . .").

CHAPTER FIVE

Influence of Spanish Literature on Shakespeare

"Amadis De Gaula"

FRENCH: *Amadis de Gaule, I-XXI,* Lyons, 1575-1581. [Books 1-8 tr. N. de Herberay; 9 tr. Gilles B[oileau] de Buillon, revised by Cl. Colet; 10, 11, 13, 14 tr. Jac. Gohorry; 12 tr. G. Aubert; 15-21 tr. Gbr. Chappuys.] Also bks. 14 and 15, tr. Ant. Tyron, Paris, 1577; bk. 16, tr. N. de Montreux, Paris, 1577; and bk. 19, tr. Jac. Charlot, Lyons, 1581.

La Thresor des douze livres d'Amadis de Gaule [no author given], Antwerp, 1560.

ITALIAN: *Amadis di Gaula* [tr. by several hands], 25 vols., Venice, 1546-1594.

GERMAN: *Hystorie von Amadis uss Franckreich,* [tr. by several hands], bks. 1-24, Frankfort on Main, 1594.

ENGLISH: *The First Book of Amadis of Gaule* [tr. from French by A. Munday, London, 1590?].

The Second Booke of Amadis of Gaule, tr. L[azarus] P[yott, i.e. Anthony Munday], London, 1595.

The Most Excellent and Pleasaunt Booke, Entituled the Treasurie of Amadis of Fraunce [tr. T. Paynell], London [1567].

Volumes XIII and following, supposedly translated from the Spanish, are believed to be original Italian works written by Mambrino Roseo.

A few surveys of Sn sources include cursory references to *Amadis of Gaul* as one of the romances S might have read.

(516)

Perott, Joseph de, "Der geniale Spitzbube bei Feliciano de Silva und Shakespeares Autolycus," *ESn,* 41 (1910): 332-333.

In the creation of Autolycus, S was influenced by the character Fraudador found in de Silva's *Amadis de Gaula.*

(517)

Perott, Joseph de, "Die Hirtendichtung des Feliciano de Silva und Shakespeares *Wintermärchen,*" *Ar,* 130 (1913) : 53-56.

Parallels are cited to prove that the source of *WT* was de Silva's *Amadis de Grecia.* A parallel is also noted between *KL,* I, iv, 79 ("Since my young lady's going into France . . .") and *Florisel de Niquea.*

(518)

Perott, Joseph de, "Spanische Einflüsse bei Shakespeare," *ESn,* 40 (1909) : 153-155.

Points of similarity are noted between *LLL* and de Silva's *Florisel de Niquea.*

(519)

Perott, Joseph de, "Eine spanische Parallele zu *Love's Labour's Lost,*" *SJ,* 44 (1908) : 151-153.

An episode in de Silva's *Libro segundo de la quarto parte de la chronica del . . . Florisel de Niquea* is paralleled in *LLL.*

(520)

Thomas, H., *Shakespeare and Spain,* The Taylorian Lecture, Oxford, 1922, pp. 21-26.

Although certain parallels suggest a possible connection between *WT* and *Amadis de Grecia,* the similarities which Joseph de Perott has pointed out between passages in S and in *Amadis de Grecia* and *Lisuarte de Grecia* are irrelevant.

"Las Burlas Veras," see **"La Española De Florencia"**

Calahorra, Diego De, see **"Espejo De Principes Y Cavalleros"**

"Calisto Y Melibea," see **"Celestina"**

"Celestina"

FRENCH: *La Celestine* [tr. J. de La Vardin], Rouen, 1598.

ITALIAN: *Celestina* [tr. Alphonso Ordognez], Rome, 1506.

GERMAN: *Ain hipsche Tragedia von zwaien liebhabenden mentschen . . . Calixstus und Melibea* [tr. C. Wirsung], Augsburg, 1520.

ENGLISH: John Rastell, *A New Comodye in Englysh . . . wherein is dyscrybed as well the bewte and good properte of women as theyr vycys* [adapted from part of *Celestina,* London], 1525.

(521)

Chandler, F. W., *The Literature of Roguery,* Boston, New York, Cambridge, 1907, p. 235 n.

Several picaresque characters in Spanish literature have been erroneously suggested as the source of Autolycus. One, the Centurio of *Celestina,* might have suggested Pistol.

(522)

Perott, Joseph de, "Falstaff und der Dreieinigkeitsbruder bei Feliciano de Silva," *Germanisch-Romanische Monatsschrift,* 2 (1910) : 633-634.

Feliciano de Silva's *Segunda Celestina* influenced S's portrayal of Falstaff in *MW* and *H4.* S's Armado is reminiscent of Felides in *Segunda Celestina.* See 523.

(523)

Thomas, H., *Shakespeare and Spain,* pp. 15-17. See 520.

There is a bare possibility that *Celestina* influenced *RJ.* Despite the suggestion of Joseph de Perott [see 522], there is no foundation for the suggestion that de Silva's *Segunda Celestina* influenced *MW.*

"Chevalier Du Soleil" is the French title for **"Espejo De Principes Y Cavalleros."**

Cota, R. De, see **"Celestina"**

DE, Spanish proper names including the prefix "de" are entered under the part of the name following the prefix; e.g., Cota, R. de.

Eslava, Antonio De

(524)

Becker, Gustav, "Zur Quellenfrage von Shakespeares *Sturm*," *SJ*, 43 (1907) : 155-168.

Tem resembles both Eslava's *Noches de invierno* and Ayrer's *Die schöne Sidea*. *Tem* contains material from each of them which is not contained in both, and both the Spanish and the German works contain material not to be found in *Tem*. Perhaps, there might have been a common source, which has not yet been found. *Tem* was not influenced by *The Mirrour of Knighthood*, despite Joseph de Perott's opinion to the contrary. See 529.

(525)

Matulka, Barbara, *The Novels of Juan of Flores and Their European Diffusion*, New York, 1931, p. 237.

Either *Noches de invierno* was the source of *Tem* or *The Mirrour of Princely Deeds and Knighthood* was a common source of *Tem* and of Eslava. The theory that *Tem* was based upon Juan de Flores' *Grisel y Mirabella* has been discarded because there is insufficient resemblance between the two.

(526)

Perott, Joseph de, "Beaumont and Fletcher and *The Mirrour of Knighthood*," *MLN*, 22 (1907) : 76-78.

Points of similarity are cited to show that *Tem* was influenced by *Noches de invierno*.

See also 461 and 470.

"La Española De Florencia" (also called **"Las Burlas Veras"**)

(527)

Luce, Morton, ed., *Rich's Apolonius and Silla: An Original of Shakespeare's Twelfth Night*, pp. 7, 44. See 464.

A possible source of *TN* was *La Española de Florencia*, author and date uncertain.

"Espejo De Principes Y Cavalleros" [**"The Mirrour Of Princely Deeds And Knighthood"**]

ENGLISH: *The Mirrour of Princely Deedes and Knighthood*, tr. M. T[yler], London [1578].

The Second Part of the First Booke of the Myrrour of Knighthood, tr. R. P.,
    London, 1585.
The Third Part of the First Booke of the Mirrour of Knighthood, tr. R. P.,
    London [1586?].
The Second Part of the Myrror of Knighthood [i.e. books 4 and 5 by P. la
    Sierra], tr. R. P., London, 1583.
The Sixth Booke of the Myrrour of Knighthood [by M. Martiñez], tr. R. P.,
    London, 1598.
The Seventh Booke of the Myrrour of Knighthood [by M. Martiñez, tr. L.
    A.], London, 1598.
The Eighth Booke of the Myrror of Knighthood [by M. Martiñez, tr. L. A.],
    London, 1599.
The Ninth Part of the Mirror of Knighthood [by M. Martiñez, no tr.], Lon-
    don, 1601.

(528)

Perott, Joseph de, *"The Mirrour of Knighthood,"* MLN, 39 (1924) : 441-
    442.

H. D. Gray's article [see 461] is criticized.

(529)

Perott, Joseph de, "The Probable Source of the Plot of Shakespeare's
    Tempest," Publications of the Clark U L, Vol. I no. 8 (1905) : 209-
    216.

From *The Mirrour of Knighthood* S obtained suggestions for *Tem,* for
Margaret's impersonation of Hero in *MA,* for Portia's Mercy Speech in *MV,*
for Mercutio's death in *RJ,* and for Ophelia's death in *H.* See 524.

(530)

Perott, Joseph de, "Der Prinzenraub aus Rache (eine *Cymbelin* Parallele),"
    SJ, 45 (1909) : 228-229.

Cym might have been dependent upon the *Mirrour of Princely Deeds and
Knighthood.*

(531)

Perott, Joseph de, "Professor Fitzmaurice-Kelly and the Source of Shake-
    speare's *Tempest,"* Romanic R, 5 (1914) : 364-367.

Fourteen passages in *Tem,* I, ii, suggest verbal dependence upon *The First
Part of the Mirrour of Princely Deeds and Knighthood.*

(532)

Perott, Joseph de, "Der Unfall im Wasser in den Wahlverwandtschaften und in dem Ritterspiegel," *Goethe Jahrbuch,* 33 (1912) : 211-214.

It is noted in passing that S made use of the fifteenth chapter of the *Mirrour of Knighthood* in describing the drowning of Ophelia.

(533)

Thomas, H., *Shakespeare and Spain,* pp. 26-30. See 520.

Joseph de Perott's suggestions to the effect that *The Mirrour of Knighthood* influenced *Tem* are unjustified. See 529 and 531.

See also 461, 524, and 525.

Flores, Juan De

La historia de Grisel y Mirabella is also known as *The History of Aurelio and Isabelle.*

SPANISH, ITALIAN, FRENCH, and ENGLISH: *Histoire de Aurelio et Isabelle: The Historie of Aurelio and of Isabell* [no tr.], Antwerp, 1556.

(534)

Matulka, Barbara, *The Novels of Juan de Flores and Their European Diffusion.* See 525.

Since *Grisel y Mirabella* and *MM* do not agree in their interpretation of the law regarding adultery, the reference to it in both works cannot be considered proof of S's dependence upon Flores. See also 525.

(535)

Perott, Joseph de, "Spanische Einflüsse bei Shakespeare." See 518.

Juan de Flores' *Historia de Grisel y Mirabella* influenced *MM,* II, iii. See 536.

(536)

Thomas, H., *Shakespeare and Spain,* pp. 17-18. See 520.

Joseph de Perott is unjustified in suggesting that *MM* was influenced by *Historia de Grisel y Mirabella.* See 535.

Hurtado De Mendoza, Diego

ENGLISH: *The Pleasaunt Historie of Lazarillo de Tormes* [sometimes attributed to D. Hurtado de Mendoza], tr. D. Rouland, London, 1586.

The Most Pleasaunt and Delectable Historie of Lazarillo de Tormes: the Second Parte, tr. W. P., London, 1596.

A number of editions of *Lazarillo de Tormes* suggest that this work influenced *MA,* II, i, 207 ff.

(537)

Chandler, F. W., *The Literature of Roguery,* pp. 233, 235 n. See 521.

S probably read *Lazarillo de Tormes* in David Rowland's translation. There is a direct allusion to this book in *MA,* II, i, 207 ff. ("Ho! now you strike like the blind man . . ."). Launcelot's practical joke at the expense of his blind father and his attempt to seek the service of a less miserly master (*MV,* II, ii) and Edgar's leading his father to jump over an imaginary cliff (*KL,* IV, vi) might also have been derived from this source.

(538)

Entwistle, W. J., "Benedick and Lazarillo," *TLS,* September 30, 1926, p. 654.

MA, II, i, 207 ff. was not influenced by *Lazarillo de Tormes.*

(539)

Hannigan, J. E., "Benedick and Lazarillo," *TLS,* September 23, 1926, p. 632.

MA, II, i, 207 ff. ("Ho! now you strike like the blind man . . .") was derived from *Lazarillo de Tormes.*

(540)

Hume, Martin, *Spanish Influence on English Literature,* London, 1905, p. 167.

The same suggestion is made as in 539.

(541)

Northup, G. T., "*The Life of Lazarillo de Tormes . . .,*" *MP,* 16 (1918-1919) : 385-389. [Pp. 388-389.]

Lazarillo de Tormes was the source from which S obtained not only *MA,* II, i, 207 ff., but also the idea of having Edgar allow his father to jump over an imaginary cliff (*KL,* IV, vi). G. T. Northup believes he is original in making this suggestion, but see 537.

(542)

Thomas, H., *Shakespeare and Spain,* p. 18. See 520.

Although there is a marked similarity between an episode in *Lazarillo de Tormes* and *MA*, II, i, 207 ff. ("Ho! now you strike like the blind man . . ."), this parallelism need be credited to nothing more than to coincidence.

"Lazarillo De Tormes," see **Hurtado De Mendoza, Diego**

Luna, Juan De, see **Hurtado De Mendoza, Diego**

Martiñez, Marcos, see **"Espejo De Principes Y Cavalleros"**

Mena, J. De, see **"Celestina"**

Mendoza, Diego Hurtado De, see **Hurtado De Mendoza, Diego**

"Mirrour Of Princely Deedes And Knighthood," see **"Espejo De Principes Y Cavalleros"**

Montemayor, Jorge De

ENGLISH: *Diana,* tr. B. Young, London, 1598.
Barnabe Googe, *Eglogs, Epytaphes, and Sonettes,* London, 1563. Eclogues 5 and 7 were derived from *Diana.*

There are Elizabethan references to other English translations in manuscript.

(543)

Ashhurst, R. L., *"The Two Gentlemen of Verona,"* New *Sna,* 3 (1904): 53-63.

Although other versions of *Diana* were available to S, he probably used Wilson's translation (which was never printed and which is not extant) for the Proteus-Julia plot of *TGV*.

(544)

Brooke, C. F. T., *The Tudor Drama,* New York, Boston, Chicago, 1911, p. 261.

Not only was *Diana* a possible source of *TGV*, but Shepherd Montano in that romance might have suggested the name of one character in *O* and of another in the older version of *H*.

(545)

Caldwell, R. M., *Shakespere's Treatment of His Sources in The Two Gentlemen of Verona*, MS Thesis, CL, 1907, 72 pp.

That *Julius und Hippolita* (or the English play upon which it was based) and some form of Montemayor's *Diana* were the sources of *TGV* is demonstrated by a careful analysis of plots and parallel passages.

(546)

Charlier, Gustave, "Sur un passage de *Comme il vous plaira* de Shakespeare," *Revue du seizième siècle*, 7 (1920) : 157-160.

Diana, generally accepted as the source of *TGV*, was suggested by Dunlop in 1814 as a source of *MND*. It also was the source of *AYL*, IV, i, 160-161 ("I will weep for nothing, like Diana in the fountain . . .").

(547)

Genouy, Hector, "Considérations sur le *Midsummer Night's Dream* de Shakespeare," *Revue de l'enseignement des langues vivantes*, 49 (1932) : 299-310. [P. 301.]

Since S was not a linguist and Young's translation did not appear until 1598, there is no justification for suggesting that *MND* was influenced by *Diana*.

(548)

Harrison, T. P. Jr., "Concerning *Two Gentlemen of Verona* and Montemayor's *Diana*," *MLN*, 41 (1926) : 251-253.

O. J. Campbell [see 458] errs in suggesting the lost English play, *Felix and Philiomena*, as the source of *TGV*. S's source was *Diana* of Montemayor.

(549)

Harrison, T. P. Jr., "Shakespeare and Montemayor's *Diana*," *Studies in English*, No. 6 (*U of Texas B*, No. 2648), 1926, pp. 72-120.

The influence of Montemayor's *Diana* on *TGV*, *MND*, and *TN* is analyzed in detail. Possible echoes of *Diana* in a number of other Sn plays and in S's *Sonnets* are also noted. No attempt is made to determine the exact version in which S read *Diana*, but Googe's *Eglogs* and the lost English play, *Felix and Philiomena* are excluded from the list of possibilities.

(550)

Henneberger, O. P., *Proximate Sources for the Italianate Elements in Shakespeare*. See 151.

TGV was derived from *Diana* rather than from plots of *commedie dell' arte*. Its structure was dependent upon that of Terence's comedy.

(551)

Reyher, Paul, "Alfred de Vigny, Shakespeare, et George de Montemayor," *Revue de l'enseignement des langues vivantes*, 37 (1920) : 1-4.

A detailed defense is offered for the suggestion that *Diana* was the source of *AYL*, IV, i, 160-161 ("I will weep for nothing, like Diana . . .").

(552)

Thomas, H., ed., *"Diana de Monte Mayor Done out of Spanish by Thomas Wilson (1596)," Revue hispanique*, 50 (1920) : 367-418.

Wilson's manuscript translation of *Diana*, I, is printed here. Although *Diana*, II, might have been the source of *TGV*, it is doubtful that S read the Spanish romance in the Wilson translation.

(553)

Tynan, J. L., "The Influence of Robert Greene on Shakspere's Early Romance," *PMLA*, 27 (1912) : 246-264.

S's deviations in *TGV* from *Diana* and from *Julius und Hippolita* or its source are briefly listed to demonstrate S's adherence to the dramatic formula of Greene.

(554)

Wales, J. G., "Shakespeare's Use of English and Foreign Elements in the Setting of *The Two Gentlemen of Verona*," p. 99. See 455.

S's allusion in *TGV* to the abbey wall (V, i, 109) might have been derived from *Diana*.

See also 458.

Ortuñez De Calahorra, Diego, see "Espejo De Principes Y Cavalleros."

Rojas, F. De, see "Celestina"

Rueda, Lope De

(555)

Leith, A. A., "New Light on *Twelfth Night*," *Baconiana*, Third Series, 2 (1904) : 103-106.

Although some scholars have suggested that Lady Clavella of *Comedia de los engañados* was the original of Lady Olivia in *TN*, Olivia is, in reality, intended to serve as a portrait of Countess Arabella, daughter of Charles Stuart.

(556)

Spens, Janet, *An Essay on Shakespeare's Relation to Tradition*, Oxford, 1916, p. 9 and 9 n.

S might have derived from Lope de Rueda the idea of having Sebastian marry Olivia at the close of *TN*.

See also 433.

Sierra, Pedro De La, see "Espejo De Principes Y Cavalleros"

Silva, Feliciano De, see "Amadis De Gaula" and "Celestina"

CHAPTER SIX

Influence of Other Foreign Literature on Shakespeare

Ayrer, Jakob

A number of critics suggest that *Tem* and *Die schöne Sidea* were both derived from the same source.

(557)

Chambers, E. K., "The Integrity of *The Tempest*." See 459.

A study of the parallels between *Die schöne Sidea* and *Tem* suggests that the arguments supporting S's dependence upon the German drama are inconclusive.

(558)

Fouquet, Karl, *Jakob Ayrers Sidea, Shakespeares Tempest, und das Märchen,* Marburg, 1929, 103 pp.

This objective study of the different folk motifs in *Tem* does not commit itself regarding the sources upon which S was actually dependent. It is demonstrated, however, that *Tem* was based not upon phantasy but upon some definite source.

(559)

Förster, Max, "Quellen," *SJ*, 49 (1913) : 233-234.

There were common sources for *CE* and Ayrer's *Comedia von zweyen Brüdern aus Syracusa,* for *MA* and *Die schöne Phoenicia,* and for *Tem* and *Die schöne Sidea*. These sources might have been English plays which are no longer extant.

See also 434, 436, 461, 524, and 561.

Duke Heinrich Julius

(560)

Bensly, Edward, "Suggested German Source of *Merry Wives of Windsor*," *NQ,* Twelfth Series, 8 (1921) : 197.

A possible source of *MW* might have been the play, *Von einem Weibe, wie dasselbige ihre Hurerei für ihren Eheman verborgen* by Duke Heinrich Julius of Brunswick. However, incidents in that play were also in existence elsewhere.

(561)

Knight, A. H. J., "Duke Heinrich Julius of Brunswick's Comedy of *Vincentius Ladislaus*," *MLR*, 34 (1939) : 50-61. [Pp. 58-60.]

The suggestion that Heinrich Julius' comedy influenced *MA* is unwarranted, nor is the case any better for Ayrer's *Die schöne Sidea* as a source of *MA*. S probably used the sources generally suggested by his critics: Ariosto, Bandello, and Spenser.

"Historie Von Vier Kaufmännern"

ENGLISH: *This Mater Treateth of a Merchauntes Wyfe That Afterwarde Went Lyke a Man and Becam a Great Lorde, and Was Called Frederyke of Jennen Afterward*, Antwerp, 1518.

(562)

Pietzker, Annemarie, *Der Kaufmann in der elisabethanischen Literatur*, Quakenbrüch, 1931, p. 15.

Not only was *Frederick of Jennen* a possible source of *MV*, but it also contains some details parallel to those in *Cym*.

See also 448 and 451.

"Julius Und Hippolita"

See 545 and 553.

Lost Dutch Play

(563)

DeVries, T[ieman], *Holland's Influence on English Language and Literature*, Chicago, 1916, pp. 275-277.

It is possible that a play on the subject of *RJ* originated in the South Netherlands. Since, if there was such a play, it has been lost, the possibility of its having influenced S's *RJ* can be no more than a hypothesis.

Leo Africanus (Hasan Ibn Muhammad, Al-Wazzan, Al-Fasi; baptised as Giovanni Leone but better known as Leo Africanus).

His work was originally written in Arabic and later translated into Italian and French.

ENGLISH: *The History and Description of Africa, and of the Notable Things Therein Contained,* tr. John Pory, London, 1600.

(564)

Whitney, Lois, "Did Shakespeare Know Leo Africanus?" *PMLA,* 37 (1922): 470-483.

Othello's character and details of his early life might easily have been obtained from Pory's version of Leo Africanus.

See also 317.

Joseph, Ben Gorion pseud.

ENGLISH: *A Compendious and Most Marveylous History of the Latter Times of the Jewes Commune Weale,* tr. P. Morwyng, London, 1561.

(565)

Gollancz, I., "Bits of Timber," pp. 171-172. See 57.

Peter Morwyng's translation of the pseudo-Josephus, which Malone suggested as the source of *KJ,* II, i, 378 ("Do like the mutines of Jerusalem . . .") contains near the beginning the names Schiloch the Babylonian and Antonius. The name "Schiloch" might have been chosen because of the erroneous association with "Schallach" the Biblical Hebrew for cormorant. In Elizabethan England the terms cormorant and usurer were synonymous.

(566)

Harris, M. D., "Note on the Mutines of Jerusalem in Shakespeare's *King John,*" *NQ,* 161 (1931): 93.

Malone noted in the Furness *Variorum* that Joseph ben Gorion might have been the source of *KJ,* II, i, 378 ("Do like the mutines of Jerusalem . . ."). S might, however, have derived the idea from John Smith's play: *The Destruction of Jerusalem,* performed by the Smiths' Craft of Coventry in 1584 and 1591.

(567)

Roth, Cecil, "The Background of Shylock," *RES,* 9 (1933) : 148-153. [P. 149.]

Shiloch the Babylonian in the chronicle by Joseph ben Gorion is cited as one of the possible sources of the name, Shylock. The names of Cush, Tubal, Shylock, and Jessica are closely paralleled by Chus, Tubal, Shelah, and Jesca of *Genesis,* X, XI.

Appendix

(568)

Galland, René, "Montaigne et Shakespeare" in *IVᵉ Centenaire de la naissance de Montaigne,* Bordeaux, 1933, pp. 333-371.

Although some of the parallels that have been urged between S and Montaigne are merely accidental, the resemblances between the philosophy of Montaigne and that mirrored in plays of the *H* period cannot be ignored.

(569)

Lefranc, Abel, *Sous le masque de William Shakespeare,* Paris, 1919, II: 251-253.

The fact that a passage in *Tem* (Gonzalo's description of the ideal commonwealth) depends upon a passage in Montaigne is used to support the thesis that the Earl of Derby was the author of the S canon.

(570)

Perott, Joseph de, "Die Vorgange im Heiligtum der Artemis zur Ephesus bei Achilles Tatios und in der Abtei daselbst bei Shakespeare," *Germanisch-Romanische Monatsschrift,* 3 (1911): 247-248.

The final scene of *CE* contains seven passages which were influenced by the last two books of Achilles Tatius.

(571)

Villey, Pierre, "Montaigne en Angleterre," *Revue des deux mondes,* 17 (1913): 115-150. [S, pp. 123-125.]

The possibility of Montaignian influence on S is considered. The writer is not so strongly opposed to that possibility here as in his later articles.

Index

Italic arabic numerals indicate *page* references.
Roman arabic numerals indicate *entry* references.
Shakespearian lines and *dramatis personae* are indexed under Shakespeare's works.

Italic arabic numerals indicate *page* references.
Roman arabic numerals indicate *entry* references.
Shakespearian lines and *dramatis personae* are indexed under Shakespeare's works.

Italic arabic numerals indicate *page* references.
Roman arabic numerals indicate *entry* references.
Shakespearian lines and *dramatis personae* are indexed under Shakespeare's works.

Italic arabic numerals indicate *page* references.
Roman arabic numerals indicate *entry* references.
Shakespearian lines and *dramatis personae* are indexed under Shakespeare's works.

Italic arabic numerals indicate *page* references.
Roman arabic numerals indicate *entry* references.
Shakespearian lines and *dramatis personae* are indexed under Shakespeare's works.

Italic arabic numerals indicate *page* references.
Roman arabic numerals indicate *entry* references.
Shakespearian lines and *dramatis personae* are indexed under Shakespeare's works.

Italic arabic numerals indicate *page* references.
Roman arabic numerals indicate *entry* references.
Shakespearian lines and *dramatis personae* are indexed under Shakespeare's works.

Italic arabic numerals indicate *page* references.
Roman arabic numerals indicate *entry* references.
Shakespearian lines and *dramatis personae* are indexed under Shakespeare's works.

Italic arabic numerals indicate *page* references.
Roman arabic numerals indicate *entry* references.
Shakespearian lines and *dramatis personae* are indexed under Shakespeare's works.

Italic arabic numerals indicate *page* references.
Roman arabic numerals indicate *entry* references.
Shakespearian lines and *dramatis personae* are indexed under Shakespeare's works.

Italic arabic numerals indicate *page* references.
Roman arabic numerals indicate *entry* references.
Shakespearian lines and *dramatis personae* are indexed under Shakespeare's works.

Italic arabic numerals indicate *page* references.
Roman arabic numerals indicate *entry* references.
Shakespearian lines and *dramatis personae* are indexed under Shakespeare's works.

Italic arabic numerals indicate *page* references.
Roman arabic numerals indicate *entry* references.
Shakespearian lines and *dramatis personae* are indexed under Shakespeare's works.

Italic arabic numerals indicate *page* references.
Roman arabic numerals indicate *entry* references.
Shakespearian lines and *dramatis personae* are indexed under Shakespeare's works.

Italic arabic numerals indicate *page* references.
Roman arabic numerals indicate *entry* references.
Shakespearian lines and *dramatis personae* are indexed under Shakespeare's works.

Italic arabic numerals indicate *page* references.
Roman arabic numerals indicate *entry* references.
Shakespearian lines and *dramatis personae* are indexed under Shakespeare's works.

Italic arabic numerals indicate *page* references.
Roman arabic numerals indicate *entry* references.
Shakespearian lines and *dramatis personae* are indexed under Shakespeare's works.

Italic arabic numerals indicate *page* references.
Roman arabic numerals indicate *entry* references.
Shakespearian lines and *dramatis personae* are indexed under Shakespeare's works.

Italic arabic numerals indicate *page* references.
Roman arabic numerals indicate *entry* references.
Shakespearian lines and *dramatis personae* are indexed under Shakespeare's works.

* When any commentary mentions a large number of Shakespearian plays, the individual plays are not named in the annotation.

Italic arabic numerals indicate *page* references.
Roman arabic numerals indicate *entry* references.
Shakespearian lines and *dramatis personae* are indexed under Shakespeare's works.

Italic arabic numerals indicate *page* references.
Roman arabic numerals indicate *entry* references.
Shakespearian lines and *dramatis personae* are indexed under Shakespeare's works.

Italic arabic numerals indicate *page* references.
Roman arabic numerals indicate *entry* references.
Shakespearian lines and *dramatis personae* are indexed under Shakespeare's works.

Italic arabic numerals indicate *page* references.
Roman arabic numerals indicate *entry* references.
Shakespearian lines and *dramatis personae* are indexed under Shakespeare's works.

Italic arabic numerals indicate *page* references.
Roman arabic numerals indicate *entry* references.
Shakesperian lines and *dramatis personae* are indexed under Shakespeare's works.

Italic arabic numerals indicate *page* references.
Roman arabic numerals indicate *entry* references.
Shakespearian lines and *dramatis personae* are indexed under Shakespeare's works.

Italic arabic numerals indicate *page* references.
Roman arabic numerals indicate *entry* references.
Shakespearian lines and *dramatis personae* are indexed under Shakespeare's works.

Italic arabic numerals indicate *page* references.
Roman arabic numerals indicate *entry* references.
Shakespearian lines and *dramatis personae* are indexed under Shakespeare's works.